The Bbq Cookbook

179 Recipes

Table Of Contents

BBQ Chicken Pizza I	1
Sweet and Tangy BBQ Sauce	2
Elaine's Sweet and Tangy Loose Beef BBQ	3
Christian's Killer BBQ and Grill Marinade	4
Oven BBQ	5
Ryan's Gourmet BBQ Sauce	6
Honey Mustard BBQ Pork Chops	7
Grilled Picante BBQ Chicken	8
Honey Garlic BBQ Sauce II	9
Simple BBQ Sauce	10
Kalbi (Korean BBQ Short Ribs)	11
Korean BBQ Short Ribs (Gal-Bi)	12
BBQ Potato Roast	13
Sweet 'n' Spicy BBQ Sauce	14
BBQ Sauce for Chicken	15
BBQ Chicken	16
Smokin' Jack BBQ Sauce	17
Firehouse BBQ Sauce	18
BBQ Feta and Hot Banana Pepper Turkey Burgers	19
Root Beer BBQ Sauce	20
BBQ Peanut Butter Chicken	21
Australian BBQ Meatballs	22
Extra Simple BBQ Banana	23
Tickety-Tock BBQ Sauce	24
BBQ Potatoes with Green Onions	25
Wildfire BBQ Beef on Buns	26
Hot and Spicy BBQ Sauce	27
BBQ Beer Brat Kabobs	28
Adult Watermelon for BBQ's	29
Slow Cooker Carolina BBQ	30
Eastern North Carolina BBQ Sauce	31
Apple and BBQ Sauce Baby Back Ribs	32
Grilled Spice Rubbed Chicken Breasts with Alabama BBQ Sauce	33
Nonie's Best BBQ	34
BBQ Glazed Homemade Meatballs	35

Table Of Contents

BBQ Meatballs	36
Vinegar Based BBQ Sauce	37
Caribbean BBQ Sauce II	38
BBQ Turkey	39
Bourbon Whiskey BBQ Sauce	40
BBQ Chicken and Bacon Bread	41
Uncle Earl's NC BBQ Sauce	42
Owen's BBQ Chicken	43
BBQ Eggs	44
BBQ Dry Rub	45
Cranberry BBQ Chicken	46
BBQ Hotdogs on Rice	47
Southern BBQ Sauce	48
Chinese Steamed Buns With BBQ Pork Filling	49
Tasty BBQ Corn on the Cob	50
Texas BBQ Chicken	51
Red BBQ Slaw	52
Scott's Savory BBQ Sauce	53
My Dad's BBQ Sauce	54
Tangy BBQ Rub	55
Carol's Spicy BBQ Sauce	56
Absolutely Awesome BBQ Sauce	57
Texas Hickory BBQ Chicken	58
White BBQ Sauce	59
Carolina BBQ Pork Sauce	60
Big John's BBQ Ribs and Dry Spice Rub	61
Oven Baked BBQ Ribs	62
BBQ Fried Chicken	63
BBQ Steak Teriyaki	64
Korean BBQ Chicken Marinade	65
BBQ Pork Sandwiches	66
Spicy BBQ Chicken	67
Korean BBQ Galbi	68
Carolina BBQ Sauce	69
Slow Cooker BBQ Pork Chops	70

Table Of Contents

Uncle Pauly's Carolina BBQ Sauce	71
BBQ Sausage and Peppers	72
BBQ Salmon over Mixed Greens	73
Canadian Barn BBQ Sauce	74
BBQ Chicken Sandwiches	75
Carolina BBQ	76
Bubba's Best BBQ Sauce	77
Slow Roasted BBQ Beef Roast	78
Kickin' BBQ Sauce	79
BBQ Chicken Pizza	80
Bob's BBQ Sauce	81
North Carolina BBQ Sauce	82
BBQ Pie	83
BBQ Chicken Wings	84
Baked BBQ Fried Chicken	85
BBQ Cola Meatballs	86
Slow Cooker BBQ Meatballs and Polish Sausage	87
BBQ Bacon Ranch Dip	88
Bulgogi (Korean BBQ)	89
Mustard Based BBQ Sauce	90
Simple BBQ Ribs	91
A Very Popular BBQ Sauce	92
Yoyo's BBQ Beans	93
Real New Orleans Style BBQ Shrimp	94
Ace's BBQ Sauce for Grilling	95
Chile Garlic BBQ Salmon	96
Easiest BBQ Pork Chops	97
Bill's Smoked BBQ Baby Back Ribs	98
BBQ Chicken Salad	99
Caribbean BBQ Sauce	100
Paul's Southern California BBQ Sauce	101
Pork BBQ	102
This and That BBQ Sauce	103
BBQ Teriyaki Pork Kabobs	104
Jack BBQ Sauce	105

Table Of Contents

BBQ Miso Chicken	106
Easy BBQ Bake	107
Carolina BBQ Peppers	108
Best BBQ Rub in Texas	109
Island BBQ Sauce	110
Slow Cooker BBQ Chicken	111
Brisket with BBQ Sauce	112
Special Honey BBQ Sauce	113
BBQ Tuna Fritters	114
BBQ Bill's Citrus Smoked Chicken	115
Big E's BBQ Rub	116
Oven BBQ Ribs	117
Easy BBQ Flank Steak with Chipotle Mayo	118
Alaskan BBQ Salmon	119
Broth Marinated BBQ Steak	120
Easy BBQ Sauce	121
Easy and Simple Korean BBQ Ribs	122
Honey Garlic BBQ Sauce	123
Mike's BBQ Chili and Honey Lamb Marinade	124
BBQ Chicken Calzones	125
Sarge's EZ Pulled Pork BBQ	126
Pam's BBQ Flat Jacks	127
Slow Cooker BBQ Flat Iron Steak Sandwiches	128
BBQ Meatballs	129
BBQ Corn	130
Best Carolina BBQ Meat Sauce	131
Quesadillas on the BBQ	132
BBQ Pork for Sandwiches	133
Fruit BBQ Marinade	134
BBQ Sauerkraut Casserole	135
Apple Radish BBQ Ribs	136
Scalloped Potatoes for the BBQ	137
Reunion BBQ's	138
Best Stovetop BBQ Ribs	139
Jbird's Authentic Sweet Vinegar BBQ Sauce	140

Table Of Contents

BBQ Country Style Ribs	141
Grant's Famous Midnight Grill BBQ Sauce	142
BBQ Nachos	143
Krystal's Perfect Marinade for BBQ or Grilled Chicken	144
BBQ Sauce to Live For	145
Slow Cooker Wieners in Wiener BBQ Sauce	146
Texas BBQ Beef Brisket	147
BBQ NY Strip	148
BBQ Steak	149
BBQ Pork Salad with Summer Fruits and Honey Balsamic	150
BBQ Sauce	151
BBQ Chili Pasta	152
Old Style BBQ Sauce	153
Dave's BBQ Sauce	154
BBQ Chicken Pizza II	155
BBQ Quesadilla	156
BBQ Pork Pizza	157
Sweet Onion BBQ Burgers	158
Delayed Heat BBQ Sauce	159
BBQ Sauce	160
BBQ Chicken Sandwiches	161
Dad's BBQ Roast	162
BBQ Sauce for Cheaters	163
Micky's Sticky Licky Sweet n Zesty BBQ Sauce	164
Tina's Best BBQ Lime Chicken	165
Grandpa Crotts BBQ Sauce	166
BBQ Chuck Roast	167
Memorial Day Best BBQ Chicken Ever!	168
Jim Goode's BBQ Beef Rub	169
Buzzsaw's BBQ Sauce	170
Blackberry BBQ Sauce	171
Kafta (BBQ)	172
Ainaa's BBQ Chicken	173
Thai Style BBQ Chicken	174
Korean BBQ Beef (Pul-Kogi)	175

Table Of Contents

Tangy BBQ Ribs	176
Easy To Do Oven BBQ Chicken	177
BBQ Beer Can Chicken	178
BBQ Rib-eye - You Won't Believe It!	179

BBQ Chicken Pizza I

Ingredients

3 boneless chicken breast halves, cooked and cubed
1 cup hickory flavored barbeque sauce
1 tablespoon honey
1 teaspoon molasses
1/3 cup brown sugar
1/2 bunch fresh cilantro, chopped
1 (12 inch) pre-baked pizza crust
1 cup smoked Gouda cheese, shredded
1 cup thinly sliced red onion

Directions

Preheat oven to 425 degrees F (220 degrees C). In a saucepan over medium high heat, combine chicken, barbeque sauce, honey, molasses, brown sugar and cilantro. Bring to a boil.

Spread chicken mixture evenly over pizza crust, and top with cheese and onions. Bake for 15 to 20 minutes, or until cheese is melted.

Sweet and Tangy BBQ Sauce

Ingredients

2 tablespoons butter
1 small onion, minced
2 cups ketchup
1/2 cup cider vinegar
1/4 cup water
1/4 cup apple juice
1/4 cup Worcestershire sauce
2 tablespoons brown sugar
2 tablespoons molasses
2 tablespoons honey
2 teaspoons dry mustard powder
1 teaspoon chili powder
1 teaspoon garlic powder
1 teaspoon ground cayenne pepper

Directions

Melt the butter in saucepan over medium heat. Stir in the onion, and cook until tender. Mix in ketchup, cider vinegar, water, apple juice, Worcestershire sauce, brown sugar, molasses, honey, mustard powder, chili powder, garlic powder, and cayenne pepper. Bring to a boil. Reduce heat to low, and simmer 30 minutes, stirring occasionally.

Elaine's Sweet and Tangy Loose Beef BBQ

Ingredients

7 pounds boneless chuck roast
1 cup water
3 tablespoons white vinegar
4 tablespoons brown sugar
2 teaspoons dry mustard
4 tablespoons Worcestershire sauce
3 cups ketchup
2 teaspoons salt
3/4 teaspoon ground black pepper
1/4 teaspoon cayenne pepper
6 cloves garlic, minced

Directions

Place the roast into a slow cooker along with the water. Cover, and cook on LOW for 2 to 4 hours, or until beef can be easily shredded with a fork.

Shred the beef, removing fat as you go. Remove 1/2 cup of the broth from the slow cooker, and reserve for later. Add the vinegar, brown sugar, dry mustard, Worcestershire sauce and ketchup. Mix in the salt, pepper, cayenne, and garlic. Stir so that the meat is well coated.

Cover, and continue to cook beef on LOW for an additional 4 to 6 hours. Add the reserved broth only if necessary to maintain moisture. Serve on toasted buns. The meat can be frozen for future use.

Christian's Killer BBQ and Grill Marinade

Ingredients

2/3 cup light olive oil
1/3 cup apple cider vinegar
1/4 cup Worcestershire sauce
1/4 cup soy sauce
1/4 cup honey
1/4 cup molasses
1/4 cup whiskey
1/3 cup seasoning salt
1/3 cup salt-free seasoning blend
1/4 cup garlic powder
1 tablespoon ginger
2 tablespoons browning sauce
2 tablespoons prepared mustard
1 tablespoon hickory-flavored liquid smoke

Directions

Place oil, vinegar, Worcestershire sauce, soy sauce, honey, molasses, whiskey, seasoning salt, salt-free seasoning blend, garlic powder, ginger, browning sauce, mustard, and liquid smoke in a resealable container or bottle, and shake well. Store marinade in refrigerator until ready to use.

Bring marinade to room temperature and shake well before each use.

Oven BBQ

Ingredients

1 pound hardwood chips
1 1/2 cups ketchup
1/2 cup brown sugar
1 (12 fluid ounce) can or bottle beer
1/4 cup distilled white vinegar
1/2 cup red wine
1/2 medium onion, diced
1 cup diced green bell pepper
1 tablespoon black pepper
1 (4 pound) whole chicken, cut into 4 pieces

Directions

Place wood chips in warm water, and soak for 2 to 3 hours.

Preheat oven to 350 degrees F (175 degrees C).

In a small saucepan, blend the ketchup, brown sugar, beer, vinegar, and wine. Mix in the onion, bell pepper, and black pepper. Simmer until thickened, approximately 10 minutes.

Spread wet wood chips evenly in the bottom of a broiler pan, adding enough water to ensure chips remain moist while cooking. Cover with broiler pan grate, and arrange chicken pieces on top. Coat chicken with the sauce, and cook approximately 1 hour, basting regularly.

In a small saucepan over medium heat, simmer any remaining sauce to be used additionally for dipping when served.

Ryan's Gourmet BBQ Sauce

Ingredients

1 cup tomato sauce
1/4 cup honey
1/4 cup soy sauce
6 tablespoons distilled white vinegar
1/4 cup light corn syrup
3 tablespoons Worcestershire sauce
2 tablespoons hoisin sauce
1/2 teaspoon cayenne pepper
salt and freshly ground black pepper to taste

Directions

In a saucepan over medium heat, mix the tomato sauce, honey, soy sauce, vinegar, corn syrup, Worcestershire sauce, hoisin sauce, cayenne pepper, salt, and pepper. Cook 30 minutes, until thickened. Cool, and use immediately.

Honey Mustard BBQ Pork Chops

Ingredients

1/3 cup honey
3 tablespoons orange juice
1 tablespoon apple cider vinegar
1 teaspoon white wine
1 teaspoon Worcestershire sauce
2 teaspoons onion powder, or to taste
1/4 teaspoon dried tarragon
3 tablespoons Dijon mustard
8 thin cut pork chops

Directions

Place honey, orange juice, vinegar, wine, Worcestershire sauce, onion powder, tarragon, and mustard in a large resealable plastic bag. Slash fatty edge of each chop in about three places without cutting into the meat; this will prevent the meat from curling during cooking. Place chops in the plastic bag, and marinate in the refrigerator for at least 2 hours.

Preheat grill for high heat.

Lightly oil grill grate. Place chops on grill, and discard marinade. Cook chops for 6 to 8 minutes, turning once, or to desired doneness.

Grilled Picante BBQ Chicken

Ingredients

3/4 cup Pace® Picante Sauce
1/4 cup barbecue sauce
6 skinless, boneless chicken breast halves

Directions

Stir the picante sauce and barbecue sauce in a small bowl. Reserve all but 1/2 cup picante sauce mixture to serve with the chicken.

Lightly oil the grill rack and heat the grill to medium. Grill the chicken for 15 minutes or until cooked through, turning and brushing often with the remaining picante sauce mixture. Discard the remaining picante sauce mixture.

Serve the chicken with the reserved picante sauce mixture.

Honey Garlic BBQ Sauce II

Ingredients

2 cups ketchup
1 bulb garlic, peeled and crushed
1 cup water
2 tablespoons hot sauce
1/4 cup honey
2 tablespoons molasses
2 tablespoons brown sugar
1 teaspoon Worcestershire sauce
1 teaspoon soy sauce
1 teaspoon salt
2 tablespoons Cajun seasoning
1 pinch paprika
1 pinch crushed red pepper
1 pinch ground white pepper
1 pinch ground black pepper
2 tablespoons cornstarch
1 tablespoon water
1/2 cup butter

Directions

In a large saucepan over medium low heat, mix together ketchup, garlic, 1 cup of water, hot sauce, honey, molasses, brown sugar, Worcestershire sauce, soy sauce, salt, Cajun seasoning, paprika, red pepper, white pepper and black pepper. Allow the mixture to simmer approximately 30 minutes.

In a small bowl, dissolve cornstarch in 1 tablespoon of water. Adjust amount of water as needed to fully dissolve cornstarch. Stir into the sauce mixture. Continue simmering approximately 15 minutes.

Stir butter into the sauce mixture. Continue simmering mixture approximately 15 more minutes, or until butter is melted and the sauce has begun to thicken. Serve over meats prepared as desired.

Simple BBQ Sauce

Ingredients

1/2 (1 ounce) package dry onion soup mix
1/2 cup packed brown sugar
2 cups ketchup
1 teaspoon Worcestershire sauce

Directions

In a medium bowl, mix together onion soup mix, sugar, ketchup, and Worcestershire sauce. Do not use until the last few minutes of cooking, because this sweet sauce will burn if cooked for too long or over too high heat.

Kalbi (Korean BBQ Short Ribs)

Ingredients

3/4 cup soy sauce
3/4 cup brown sugar
3/4 cup water
1 garlic clove, minced
2 green onions, chopped
1 tablespoon Asian (toasted) sesame oil
2 pounds Korean-style short ribs (beef chuck flanken, cut 1/3 to 1/2 inch thick across bones)

Directions

In a bowl, stir together the soy sauce, brown sugar, water, garlic, green onions, and sesame oil until the sugar has dissolved.

Place the ribs in a large plastic zipper bag. Pour the marinade over the ribs, squeeze out all the air, and refrigerate the bag for 3 hours to overnight.

Preheat an outdoor grill for medium-high heat, and lightly oil the grate. Remove the ribs from the bag, shake off the excess marinade, and discard the marinade. Grill the ribs on the preheated grill until the meat is still pink but not bloody nearest the bone, 5 to 7 minutes per side.

Korean BBQ Short Ribs (Gal-Bi)

Ingredients

3/4 cup soy sauce
3/4 cup water
3 tablespoons white vinegar
1/4 cup dark brown sugar
2 tablespoons white sugar
1 tablespoon black pepper
2 tablespoons sesame oil
1/4 cup minced garlic
1/2 large onion, minced
3 pounds Korean-style short ribs (beef chuck flanken, cut 1/3 to 1/2 inch thick across bones)

Directions

Pour soy sauce, water, and vinegar into a large, non-metallic bowl. Whisk in brown sugar, white sugar, pepper, sesame oil, garlic, and onion until the sugars have dissolved. Submerge the ribs in this marinade, and cover with plastic wrap. Refrigerate 7 to 12 hours; the longer, the better.

Preheat an outdoor grill for medium-high heat.

Remove ribs from the marinade, shake off excess, and discard the marinade. Cook on preheated grill until the meat is no longer pink, 5 to 7 minutes per side.

BBQ Potato Roast

Ingredients

10 potatoes, peeled and halved
1/2 cup vegetable oil
2 tablespoons seasoned salt

Directions

Preheat grill for high heat.

Place potatoes in a large saucepan with enough lightly salted water to cover. Bring to a boil. Cook 15 minutes, or until tender but firm.

Drain potatoes, and pat dry. Coat thoroughly with vegetable oil and seasoned salt.

Place potatoes on the preheated grill. Cook approximately 20 minutes, turning periodically.

Sweet 'n' Spicy BBQ Sauce

Ingredients

2 cups packed brown sugar
2 cups ketchup
1 cup water
1 cup cider vinegar
1 cup finely chopped onion
1 (8 ounce) can tomato sauce
1 cup corn syrup
1 cup molasses
1 (6 ounce) can tomato paste
2 tablespoons Worcestershire sauce
1 tablespoon garlic pepper blend
1 tablespoon liquid smoke flavoring (optional)
1 tablespoon prepared mustard
1 teaspoon onion salt
1 teaspoon celery salt

Directions

In a large saucepan, combine all ingredients. Bring to a boil. Reduce heat; simmer, uncovered, for 15 minutes or until the flavors are blended. Remove from the heat; cool.

BBQ Sauce for Chicken

Ingredients

3 tablespoons vegetable oil
2 onions, chopped
5 cloves garlic, minced
1 (12 fluid ounce) can frozen orange juice concentrate, thawed
2 teaspoons mustard powder
2 cups ketchup
1 lemon, juiced
1/2 cup Burgundy wine
salt and pepper to taste

Directions

In a medium skillet saute onion and garlic for 4 to 5 minutes (until translucent). Add the orange juice, mustard, ketchup, lemon, Chianti/burgundy, salt and pepper. Simmer all together over low heat for 30 minutes, then put through food processor. Sauce may be thinned with water to taste, if desired.

BBQ Chicken

Ingredients

3 tablespoons vegetable oil
1 1/2 cups cider vinegar
1 tablespoon salt
1/4 teaspoon ground black pepper
2 teaspoons poultry seasoning
2 pounds cut up chicken pieces

Directions

Heat grill to medium heat.

In a small skillet combine the oil, vinegar, salt and pepper and put over low heat. Add the poultry seasoning while stirring constantly; when sauce mixes well and starts to bubble, it is done.

Place chicken on hot grill and brush with sauce. Grill for 45 to 60 minutes, turning every 5 to 10 minutes, and brush chicken with sauce after each turning. Grill until chicken is done and juices run clear. (Note: Be sure to keep an eye on the chicken as it cooks, as it tends to have flair ups due to the oil and chicken drippings!)

Smokin' Jack BBQ Sauce

Ingredients

8 cups ketchup
6 ounces chipotle peppers in adobo sauce
1/2 cup apple cider vinegar
1/2 cup molasses
1 1/2 teaspoons onion powder
1 1/2 teaspoons garlic powder
1 1/2 teaspoons ground mustard
1 1/2 teaspoons smoked paprika
1 1/2 teaspoons ground coriander
1 tablespoon kosher salt
1 1/2 teaspoons freshly cracked black pepper
1 cup dark brown sugar
1 cup whiskey (such as Jack Daniels®)
2 tablespoons liquid hickory smoke flavoring

Directions

Combine the ketchup, chipotle peppers in their sauce, apple cider vinegar, molasses, onion powder, garlic powder, ground mustard, smoked paprika, coriander, salt, black pepper, brown sugar, whiskey, and liquid smoke flavoring in a large pot, and bring to a gentle boil over medium heat, stirring frequently. Cook the sauce for 15 minutes, then reduce heat to low and simmer 15 more minutes, stirring often. Use immediately or refrigerate.

Firehouse BBQ Sauce

Ingredients

1 (46 fluid ounce) bottle ketchup
1 1/2 cups apple cider vinegar
2 cups packed brown sugar
1/2 cup butter, cut into pieces
2 tablespoons red pepper flakes, or to taste

Directions

Pour ketchup into a large saucepan. Pour vinegar into the ketchup bottle, shake to loosen any remaining ketchup, and pour into the saucepan. Save the bottle, and clean. Stir in the brown sugar, butter, and red pepper flakes. Cook over medium heat until almost boiling, but do not boil. For convenience, refrigerate leftover sauce in the clean ketchup bottle.

BBQ Feta and Hot Banana Pepper Turkey Burgers

Ingredients

1 pound ground turkey
1/4 cup seeded, chopped banana peppers
1/2 cup crumbled feta cheese
salt and pepper to taste

Directions

Preheat an outdoor grill for high heat.

In a bowl, mix the turkey, peppers, and feta cheese. Season with salt and pepper. Form the mixture into 4 patties.

Cook patties about 8 minutes per side on the prepared grill, to an internal temperature of 180 degrees F (85 degrees C).

Root Beer BBQ Sauce

Ingredients

2 cups root beer
2 cups ketchup
1/2 cup no-pulp orange juice
1/4 cup Worcestershire sauce
1/4 cup molasses
1 teaspoon ground ginger
1 teaspoon hot paprika
1 teaspoon chipotle chile powder
2 teaspoons garlic powder
2 teaspoons onion powder
1/2 teaspoon crushed red pepper flakes

Directions

Stir together the root beer, ketchup, orange juice, Worcestershire sauce, and molasses in a saucepan. Season with ginger, paprika, chipotle powder, garlic powder, onion powder, and red pepper flakes. Bring to a boil over high heat, then reduce heat to medium-low and simmer 15 minutes, stirring occasionally. Use immediately or store in the refrigerator up to a week.

BBQ Peanut Butter Chicken

Ingredients

1 cup SMUCKER'S® Natural Peanut Butter
1/4 cup soy sauce
1/4 cup white wine vinegar
1/4 cup lemon juice
6 cloves garlic, chopped
1 teaspoon red pepper flakes
2 teaspoons ginger, finely chopped
2 1/2 pounds chicken breasts, boneless and skinless, cut into 1 1/2-inch strips.

Directions

Prepare marinade 2 hours before ready to grill.

Mix the ingredients, except the chicken in a blender until combined. If too thick, add up to a cup of water to thin.

Marinate the chicken for approximately 2 hours.

Lightly oil the medium/hot BBQ grill.

Place chicken on the grill for 6-8 minutes.

Australian BBQ Meatballs

Ingredients

1 pound ground beef
1/2 cup bread crumbs
2 small onions, chopped
1 tablespoon curry powder
1 tablespoon dried Italian seasoning
1 egg, beaten
1 clove garlic, minced
1/2 cup milk
1/2 teaspoon salt
1/2 teaspoon ground black pepper

1 tablespoon margarine
2 small onions, chopped
3/4 cup ketchup
1/2 cup beef stock
1/4 cup steak sauce
1/2 cup Worcestershire sauce
2 tablespoons white vinegar
2 tablespoons instant coffee granules
1/2 cup packed brown sugar
3 tablespoons lemon juice

Directions

Preheat the oven to 375 degrees F (190 degrees C). In a medium bowl, mix together the ground beef, bread crumbs, 2 onions, curry powder, Italian seasoning, egg, garlic, salt and pepper. Gradually mix in the milk until you have a nice texture for forming meatballs. You may not need all of the milk. Form the meat into balls slightly smaller than golf balls. Place them in a greased baking dish.

Bake the meatballs for 30 minutes in the preheated oven. Once the meatballs are in the oven, start making the sauce straight away.

Melt the margarine in a saucepan over medium heat. Add the remaining onions, and cook until browned. Stir in the ketchup, beef stock, steak sauce, Worcestershire sauce, vinegar, instant coffee, brown sugar and lemon juice. Bring to a boil over medium heat, and simmer, stirring occasionally, until the meatballs are done.

Remove the meatballs from the oven, and drain any excess grease. Pour the sauce over them, and return to the oven. Bake for an additional 30 minutes.

These meatballs taste even better after they have been left to rest for a while to soak up the sauce. I usually make the recipe at lunchtime and let it cool. I put it back in the oven at about 200 degrees for approximately 15 minutes to reheat for dinner. This is not necessary but it makes it taste even better!

Extra Simple BBQ Banana

Ingredients

2 bananas
4 scoops vanilla ice cream
1 teaspoon chopped fresh mint (optional)

Directions

Place whole, unpeeled bananas on grill, turning occasionally until the peel is blackened. Remove stems and skin.

Slice bananas, and serve over vanilla ice cream with mint garnish.

Tickety-Tock BBQ Sauce

Ingredients

1 (12 ounce) bottle barbeque sauce
1/2 cup apple cider vinegar
1/4 cup ketchup
2 tablespoons stone ground horseradish mustard

Directions

In a saucepan, combine the barbeque sauce, cider vinegar, ketchup, and horseradish mustard. Bring to a boil and cook for 1 minute. Use with your favorite barbequed meat.

BBQ Potatoes with Green Onions

Ingredients

6 large potatoes, peeled
4 green onions, finely chopped
2 tablespoons butter
salt and ground black pepper to taste

Directions

Preheat an outdoor grill for high heat.

Microwave potatoes on High 5 to 8 minutes, until tender but still firm. Cool slightly, and cube.

Place cubed potatoes on a large piece of foil. Top with green onions. Dot with butter, and season with salt and pepper. Tightly seal foil around the potatoes.

Cook on the prepared grill 20 to 30 minutes, until tender.

Wildfire BBQ Beef on Buns

Ingredients

3 pounds chuck roast or round steak
1 small onion, thinly sliced
1 cup Bob Evans® Wildfire BBQ Sauce
1/2 cup apricot preserves
2 tablespoons Dijon mustard
12 rolls or buns

Directions

Place beef and onion into slow cooker. Combine Wildfire sauce, preserves and mustard and pour into slow cooker. Cover and heat on low for 8 to 10 hours or until meat is tender. Remove meat and shred with 2 forks. Combine shredded meat with sauce and serve on buns.

Hot and Spicy BBQ Sauce

Ingredients

1 (46 fluid ounce) bottle ketchup
2 cups apple cider vinegar
1 cup SPLENDA® No Calorie Sweetener, Granulated
1/2 cup butter
1 tablespoon red pepper flakes
1/4 cup Texas style hot sauce

Directions

In a large saucepan or soup pot, stir together the ketchup, cider vinegar, SPLENDA® Granulated Sweetener, butter, red pepper flakes and hot sauce. Cook over medium heat until the butter is melted and the sauce is heated through.

BBQ Beer Brat Kabobs

Ingredients

1 (19 ounce) package Bob EvansB® Beer Bratwurst, cut into 1-inch pieces
1 green bell pepper, cut into 1-inch pieces
1 medium zucchini, cut into 1-inch pieces
1 red bell pepper, cut into 1-inch pieces
1 medium yellow squash, cut into 1-inch pieces
2 cups fresh button mushroom caps
1 medium red onion, cut into 1-inch pieces
2 cups Bob EvansB® Wildfire BBQ Sauce
6 (10 inch) wooden skewers

Directions

Soak wooden skewers in water 30 minutes. Alternately thread bratwurst and vegetables onto skewers. Grill or broil kabobs 12 to 15 minutes or until brats are cooked through, turning and brushing occasionally with barbecue sauce. Refrigerate leftovers.

Adult Watermelon for BBQ's

Ingredients

1 seedless watermelon
1 1/2 cups rum, or as needed

Directions

Rinse the outer rind of the watermelon thoroughly, and pat dry. Set the watermelon in a position so it will not roll over. Press the tip of a funnel through the rind of the melon. If using a plastic funnel, you may need to cut a hole.

Situate the melon on a towel in the bottom of the refrigerator or on the counter. Pour rum into the funnel a little at a time, refilling as it seeps into the melon. I start the afternoon before, since we usually leave to go to events in the morning. Allow the melon to marinate at least a few hours, before removing the funnel. Slice just before serving.

Slow Cooker Carolina BBQ

Ingredients

1 (5 pound) bone-in pork shoulder roast
1 tablespoon salt
ground black pepper
1 1/2 cups apple cider vinegar
2 tablespoons brown sugar
1 1/2 tablespoons hot pepper sauce
2 teaspoons cayenne pepper
2 teaspoons crushed red pepper flakes

Directions

Place the pork shoulder into a slow cooker and season with salt and pepper. Pour the vinegar around the pork. Cover, and cook on Low for 12 hours. Pork should easily pull apart into strands.

Remove the pork from the slow cooker and discard any bones. Strain out the liquid, and save 2 cups. Discard any extra. Shred the pork using tongs or two forks, and return to the slow cooker. Stir the brown sugar, hot pepper sauce, cayenne pepper, and red pepper flakes into the reserved sauce. Mix into the pork in the slow cooker. Cover and keep on Low setting until serving.

Eastern North Carolina BBQ Sauce

Ingredients

1 cup white vinegar
1 cup cider vinegar
1 tablespoon brown sugar
1 tablespoon cayenne pepper
1 tablespoon hot pepper sauce (e.g. Tabascoв„ў), or to taste
1 teaspoon salt
1 teaspoon ground black pepper

Directions

Combine the white vinegar, cider vinegar, brown sugar, cayenne pepper, hot pepper sauce, salt and pepper in a jar or bottle with a tight-fitting lid. Refrigerate for 1 to 2 days before using so that the flavors will blend. Shake occasionally, and store for up to 2 months in the refrigerator.

Apple and BBQ Sauce Baby Back Ribs

Ingredients

4 cups barbeque sauce
4 cups applesauce
4 pounds baby back pork ribs
salt and black pepper to taste
cayenne pepper to taste
garlic powder to taste

Directions

Mix the barbeque sauce and applesauce in bowl. Place ribs on a large sheet of heavy duty aluminum foil, and rub on all sides with the salt, pepper, cayenne pepper, and garlic powder. Pour sauce over ribs to coat. Seal ribs in the foil. Marinate in the refrigerator 8 hours, or overnight.

Preheat grill for high heat.

Place ribs in foil on the grill grate, and cook 1 hour. Remove ribs from foil, and place directly on the grill grate. Continue cooking 30 minutes, basting frequently with the sauce, until ribs are done.

Grilled Spice Rubbed Chicken Breasts with

Ingredients

1 cup Hellmann's® or Best Foods® Real Mayonnaise
2 tablespoons cider vinegar
2 tablespoons horseradish
1/8 teaspoon cayenne chili powder
4 (6 ounce) boneless, skinless chicken breasts
2 tablespoons canola oil
2 tablespoons Bobby Flay's Sixteen Spice Rub for Poultry or your favorite spice rub or grill seasoning

Directions

Combine Hellmann's® or Best Foods® Real Mayonnaise, vinegar, horseradish and chili powder in small bowl. Season, if desired, with salt and pepper; reserve 1/2 cup sauce and set aside.

Brush chicken on both sides with oil and season, if desired, with salt and pepper. Evenly sprinkle top of chicken with spice rub.

Grill chicken, rub-side down, until golden brown and crust has formed, about 4 minutes. Brush chicken with mayonnaise mixture, turn over and cook an additional 4 minutes or until chicken is thoroughly cooked. Remove to serving platter, then cover loosely with aluminum foil and let sit 5 minutes before serving. Slice each breast and serve with reserved 1/2 cup sauce on the side.

Nonie's Best BBQ

Ingredients

1 (14 ounce) bottle ketchup
1/2 cup water
1/4 cup white sugar
1 tablespoon brown sugar
1 tablespoon red wine vinegar
1 tablespoon prepared yellow mustard
1 teaspoon salt
1/4 teaspoon ground black pepper
1/4 teaspoon paprika
2 pounds ground beef
2 teaspoons minced onion
12 hamburger buns, split

Directions

Whisk together the ketchup, water, white sugar, brown sugar, vinegar, mustard, salt, pepper, and paprika in a large saucepan. Bring to a simmer over medium-high heat; reduce heat to medium-low and simmer 15 minutes.

Meanwhile, heat a large skillet over medium-high heat; cook and stir the ground beef and onion in the hot skillet until the beef is crumbly, evenly browned, and no longer pink; drain and discard any excess grease. Stir the beef into the simmering barbeque sauce. Simmer together for 10 minutes. Spoon into the buns to serve.

BBQ Glazed Homemade Meatballs

Ingredients

1 1/2 pounds ground beef
1 egg, lightly beaten
1 cup quick cooking oats
6 1/2 ounces evaporated milk
1 teaspoon salt
1/4 teaspoon pepper
1/2 teaspoon garlic powder
1 tablespoon chili powder
1/2 cup chopped onion

1 cup ketchup
1/4 teaspoon minced garlic
1 cup brown sugar
1/4 cup chopped onion
1 tablespoon liquid smoke flavoring

Directions

Preheat oven to 350 degrees F (175 degrees C). Lightly grease a medium baking dish.

In a bowl, mix beef, egg, oats, evaporated milk, salt, pepper, garlic powder, chili powder, and 1/2 cup onion. Form into 1 1/2 inch balls and arrange in a single layer in the baking dish.

In a separate bowl, mix ketchup, garlic, sugar, 1/4 cup onion, and liquid smoke. Pour evenly over the meatballs.

Bake uncovered 1 hour in the preheated oven, until the minimum internal temperature of a meatball reaches 160 degrees F (72 degrees C).

BBQ Meatballs

Ingredients

4 eggs, beaten
1/2 cup vodka
1/2 cup water
1 tablespoon Worcestershire sauce
2 tablespoons dried minced onion flakes
1 teaspoon garlic powder, or to taste
1/2 teaspoon salt, or to taste
1/2 teaspoon ground black pepper, or to taste
3 pounds ground beef
2 pounds ground turkey
1 (15 ounce) package Italian seasoned bread crumbs

2 (28 ounce) cans crushed tomatoes
2 (14.25 ounce) cans tomato puree
1 (18 ounce) bottle hickory smoke flavored barbeque sauce
1 (8 ounce) can crushed pineapple
1 cup brown sugar
1 (14 ounce) bottle ketchup
1/2 cup vodka
2 tablespoons dried minced onion flakes
1 teaspoon garlic powder, or to taste
1/2 teaspoon salt, or to taste
1/2 teaspoon ground black pepper, or to taste

Directions

In a large bowl, combine eggs, 1/2 cup vodka and Worcestershire sauce. Season with 2 tablespoons onion flakes, garlic powder, salt and pepper. Mix in ground beef, ground turkey and bread crumbs. Shape into meatballs, and set aside.

In a very large pot over medium heat, Combine crushed tomatoes, tomato puree, barbeque sauce, pineapple, brown sugar, ketchup, and 1/2 cup vodka. Season to taste with onion flakes, garlic powder, salt and pepper. Bring to a boil, reduce heat and let simmer.

Heat a large heavy skillet over medium heat. Cook meatballs until evenly brown on all sides. Carefully place into sauce, and simmer for at least an hour.

Vinegar Based BBQ Sauce

Ingredients

1 cup cider vinegar
1 tablespoon salt
1/2 teaspoon cayenne pepper
1 teaspoon crushed red pepper flakes
1 tablespoon brown sugar

Directions

In a small bowl, combine the vinegar, salt, cayenne pepper, crushed red pepper flakes and brown sugar. Mix well and allow ingredients to mesh for about 4 to 8 hours before using.

Caribbean BBQ Sauce II

Ingredients

2 tablespoons olive oil
1 cup minced onion
2 cloves garlic, minced
3 (1 inch) pieces fresh ginger root, minced
2 cups ketchup
1/2 cup brown sugar
1/4 cup molasses
1/2 cup spiced rum, divided
3 tablespoons hoisin sauce
2 tablespoons tomato paste
2 tablespoons sherry vinegar
1 tablespoon chili powder
1/8 teaspoon cayenne pepper

Directions

Heat the olive oil in a saucepan over medium-high heat. Stir in the onion, garlic, and ginger, and cook until tender. Reduce heat to low. Mix in ketchup, brown sugar, molasses, rum, hoisin sauce, tomato paste, vinegar, chili powder, and cayenne pepper. Cook and stir 5 minutes, until well blended and heated through. Stir in remaining rum.

BBQ Turkey

Ingredients

2 cups butter, divided
1 (15 pound) whole turkey, neck and giblets removed
1/4 cup chicken soup base
3 sweet onions, peeled and cut into wedges
5 apples, cored and cut into wedges
2 tablespoons minced garlic, or to taste
1 (750 milliliter) bottle dry white wine

Directions

Preheat a gas grill for low heat.

Rub some of the butter all over the turkey, inside and out, then rub all over with chicken base. Cut remaining butter into cubes and toss with onions, apples, and garlic in a large bowl. Stuff the bird with this mixture and place in a disposable aluminum roasting pan. Fold the turkey skin around the neck area to cover the hole and then turn the turkey over and pour wine into the opening at the other end until the turkey is full or the bottle is empty. Set the turkey breast side up.

Place the roasting pan on the grill and cover loosely with aluminum foil. If you have a pop up timer or heat safe meat thermometer, insert it into the turkey breast. Close the lid.

Roast until the temperature in the breast reads 170 degrees F (75 degrees C) and the temperature in the thickest part of the thigh reads 180 degrees C (80 degrees C), about 4 hours depending on the temperature of your grill. When the temperature is getting close, remove the aluminum foil covering the turkey and allow it to brown during the final minutes of cooking. If it starts to brown too much, just cover it back up. Allow the turkey to rest for at least 20 minutes before carving.

Bourbon Whiskey BBQ Sauce

Ingredients

1/2 onion, minced
4 cloves garlic, minced
3/4 cup bourbon whiskey
1/2 teaspoon ground black pepper
1/2 tablespoon salt
2 cups ketchup
1/4 cup tomato paste
1/3 cup cider vinegar
2 tablespoons liquid smoke flavoring
1/4 cup Worcestershire sauce
1/2 cup packed brown sugar
1/3 teaspoon hot pepper sauce, or to taste

Directions

In a large skillet over medium heat, combine the onion, garlic, and whiskey. Simmer for 10 minutes, or until onion is translucent. Mix in the ground black pepper, salt, ketchup, tomato paste, vinegar, liquid smoke, Worcestershire sauce, brown sugar, and hot pepper sauce.

Bring to a boil. Reduce heat to medium-low, and simmer for 20 minutes. Run sauce through a strainer if you prefer a smooth sauce.

BBQ Chicken and Bacon Bread

Ingredients

1 egg
1/4 cup water
3 cooked skinless, boneless chicken breast halves, chopped
6 slices bacon - cooked and crumbled
1 small green bell pepper, chopped
1 1/2 cups honey barbecue sauce, divided
1 (8 ounce) package shredded Cheddar-Monterey Jack cheese blend, divided
all-purpose flour for rolling
1 (11.5 ounce) can refrigerated crusty French loaf dough

Directions

Preheat an oven to 350 degrees F (175 degrees C). Whisk egg and water; set aside.

Combine chicken, bacon, bell pepper, 1 cup barbecue sauce, and 1 cup of shredded cheese blend. The barbecue sauce should coat the meat; if the mixture is too dry, add more sauce.

Unroll dough on smooth, clean, well-floured surface, and spread or roll out to 1/4 inch thick, keeping rectangular shape. Spread the chicken mixture down the middle of the dough. Top the mixture with more barbecue sauce and the rest of the cheese. Fold one side of dough over mixture. Brush egg wash on edge of folded dough; then fold over other side of dough, sealing with egg wash. Seal both ends of loaf well with egg wash and brush it over the top of the bread.

Carefully place the bread on a greased baking sheet. Bake in the preheated oven until golden brown, about 25 to 35 minutes. Cool slightly before slicing.

Uncle Earl's NC BBQ Sauce

Ingredients

1 (46 fluid ounce) bottle ketchup
2 cups apple cider vinegar
1 cup white sugar
1/2 cup butter
1 tablespoon red pepper flakes
1/4 cup Texas style hot sauce

Directions

In a large saucepan or soup pot, stir together the ketchup, cider vinegar, sugar, butter, red pepper flakes and hot sauce. Cook over medium heat until the butter is melted and the sauce is heated through. Use right away, or store in the refrigerator for up to a month.

Owen's BBQ Chicken

Ingredients

2 tablespoons vegetable oil
1 onion, finely chopped
2 cloves crushed garlic
3/4 cup ketchup
2 tablespoons Worcestershire sauce
2 tablespoons white wine vinegar
2 tablespoons brown sugar
1/2 cup water
salt and pepper to taste
10 chicken legs

Directions

Heat oil in a medium saucepan over medium heat. Add the onion and garlic and saute for 5 to 10 minutes, or until onion is tender. Then add the ketchup, Worcestershire sauce, vinegar, brown sugar and water. Mix together well and season with salt and pepper to taste. Reduce heat to low, cover and simmer for 20 minutes. Set aside, covered, and let cool.

Place chicken in a shallow, nonporous dish and pour sauce over chicken, reserving some sauce in a separate container for basting. Cover chicken and marinate in the refrigerator for at least one hour, or overnight. Cover reserved sauce, if any, and keep in the refrigerator.

Preheat an outdoor grill for medium high heat and lightly oil grate.

Grill chicken over medium high heat for 8 to 12 minutes per side, basting occasionally with the sauce, if any, until internal temperature reaches 180 degrees F (80 degrees C).

BBQ Eggs

Ingredients

4 eggs
2 1/2 tablespoons barbecue sauce
2 tablespoons milk
1 1/2 teaspoons dried dill
1 1/2 teaspoons mustard powder
1 1/2 teaspoons minced garlic
1 tablespoon butter or margarine
1/2 cup shredded Cheddar cheese

Directions

In a medium bowl, whisk together the eggs, barbeque sauce, milk, dill, mustard powder and garlic.

Melt butter or margarine in a large skillet over medium heat. Pour in the egg mixture, and cook stirring frequently until eggs are scrambled and cooked through. Remove from heat, and sprinkle cheese over the top. Let stand for a minute to melt cheese, then serve immediately.

BBQ Dry Rub

Ingredients

1 1/4 cups white sugar
1 1/4 cups brown sugar
1/2 cup salt
1/4 cup freshly ground black pepper
1/4 cup paprika

Directions

In a medium bowl, mix together white and brown sugars, salt, pepper, and paprika. Rub onto pork 10 minutes prior to grilling. Store any leftover rub in a sealed container.

Cranberry BBQ Chicken

Ingredients

1 (2 to 3 pound) whole chicken, cut into pieces
2 tablespoons butter
1/2 teaspoon salt
1/4 teaspoon ground black pepper
1/2 cup chopped celery
1 onion, chopped
1 (16 ounce) can whole cranberry sauce
1 cup barbecue sauce

Directions

Preheat oven to 350 degrees F (175 degrees C).

In a large skillet brown the chicken in butter/margarine. Season with salt and pepper. Remove from skillet and place in a lightly greased 9x13 inch baking dish.

In the drippings (in the skillet), saute onion and celery until tender. Add cranberry sauce and barbecue sauce. Mix well.

Pour cranberry mixture over chicken and bake in the preheated oven for 90 minutes, basting every 15 minutes.

BBQ Hotdogs on Rice

Ingredients

1 cup uncooked long grain white rice
2 cups water
1 pound kielbasa sausage, thinly sliced
1/2 cup dark molasses
2 tablespoons distilled white vinegar
1 (10 ounce) can tomato sauce
1/4 cup barbeque sauce (optional)

Directions

Place the rice and water in a pot, and bring to a boil. Reduce heat to low, cover, and simmer 20 minutes.

Cook the kielbasa in a skillet over medium heat until evenly browned. Mix in the molasses, vinegar, tomato sauce, and barbeque sauce. Continue to cook until heated through. Serve over the rice.

Southern BBQ Sauce

Ingredients

1 1/4 gallons apple cider vinegar
1 (28 ounce) bottle ketchup
5 1/2 ounces chili pepper flakes
4 ounces cayenne pepper
2 ounces ground black pepper
3 ounces ground paprika

Directions

In a large, clean tub, mix together the cider vinegar and ketchup. Season with chili flakes, cayenne pepper, black pepper, and paprika. Mix well, and store in air tight containers. This does not need to be cooked.

Chinese Steamed Buns With BBQ Pork Filling

Ingredients

1/2 pound boneless pork loin roast
1/2 cup barbecue sauce
3 tablespoons shallots, chopped
1/3 cup chicken broth
1 tablespoon dark soy sauce
1 tablespoon vegetable oil
1 tablespoon white sugar
1 recipe Chinese Steamed Buns

Directions

Mix together pork, barbecue sauce, shallots, flour, chicken stock, soy sauce, oil, and sugar. Chill in refrigerator for at least 6 hours.

Prepare dough for Chinese Steamed Buns.

Shape dough into balls. Roll each out into a circle, (like Won-Ton wrappers). Put 1 tablespoonful of prepared meat mixture in the center of each circle, and wrap dough around filling. Place seams down onto wax paper squares.   Let stand until doubled, about 30 minutes.

Bring water to a boil in wok, and reduce heat to medium; the water should still be boiling. Place steam-plate on a small wire rack in the middle of the wok. Transfer as many buns on wax paper as will comfortably fit onto steam-plate leaving 1 to 2 inches between the buns. At least 2 inches space should be left between steam-plate and the wok. Cover wok with lid. Steam buns over boiling water for 15 to 20 minutes.

REMOVE LID BEFORE you turn off heat, or else water will drip back onto bun surface and produce yellowish "blisters" on bun surfaces. Continue steaming batches of buns until all are cooked.

Tasty BBQ Corn on the Cob

Ingredients

1 teaspoon chili powder
1/8 teaspoon dried oregano
1 pinch onion powder
cayenne pepper to taste
garlic powder to taste
salt and pepper to taste
1/2 cup butter, softened
6 ears corn, husked and cleaned

Directions

Preheat grill for medium-high heat.

In a medium bowl, mix together the chili powder, oregano, onion powder, cayenne pepper, garlic powder, salt, and pepper. Blend in the softened butter. Apply this mixture to each ear of corn, and place each ear onto a piece of aluminum foil big enough to wrap the corn. Wrap like a burrito, and twist the ends to close.

Place wrapped corn on the preheated grill, and cook 20 to 30 minutes, until tender when poked with a fork. Turn corn occasionally during cooking.

Texas BBQ Chicken

Ingredients

8 boneless, skinless chicken breast halves
3 tablespoons brown sugar
1 tablespoon ground paprika
1 teaspoon salt
1 teaspoon dry mustard
1/2 teaspoon chili powder
1/4 cup distilled white vinegar
1/8 teaspoon cayenne pepper
2 tablespoons Worcestershire sauce
1 1/2 cups tomato-vegetable juice cocktail
1/2 cup ketchup
1/4 cup water
2 cloves garlic, minced

Directions

Preheat the oven to 350 degrees F (175 degrees C).

Place the chicken breasts in a single layer in a 9x13 inch baking dish. In a medium bowl, mix together the brown sugar, paprika, salt, dry mustard, chili powder, vinegar, cayenne pepper, Worcestershire sauce, vegetable juice cocktail, ketchup, water and garlic. Pour the sauce evenly over the chicken breasts.

Bake uncovered, for 35 minutes in the preheated oven. Remove chicken breasts, shred with a fork, and return to the sauce. Bake in the oven for an additional 10 minutes so the chicken can soak up more flavor. Serve on a bed of rice with freshly ground black pepper.

Red BBQ Slaw

Ingredients

4 cups finely shredded cabbage
1/3 cup apple cider vinegar
1/3 cup ketchup
2 tablespoons white sugar
2 teaspoons crushed red pepper flakes, or to taste
2 dashes hot pepper sauce, or to taste

Directions

Place the cabbage into a salad bowl. In a small bowl, whisk together apple cider vinegar, ketchup, sugar, red pepper flakes, and hot sauce until the sugar has dissolved. Pour the dressing over the cabbage, toss thoroughly, and refrigerate at least 1 hour before serving.

Scott's Savory BBQ Sauce

Ingredients

1 quart apple cider vinegar
1 (20 ounce) bottle ketchup
1/4 cup paprika
1 pound dark brown sugar
1/4 cup salt
1 tablespoon black pepper
2 tablespoons red pepper flakes
1 tablespoon garlic powder
1/4 cup Worcestershire sauce
1/2 cup lemon juice

Directions

In a large container, mix together the apple cider vinegar, ketchup, paprika, brown sugar, salt, pepper, red pepper flakes, garlic powder, Worcestershire sauce and lemon juice. Pour into an empty vinegar bottle, ketchup bottle or other container and store in the refrigerator for up to 1 month.

My Dad's BBQ Sauce

Ingredients

2 cups barbeque sauce
2 cups red wine
2 tablespoons onion powder
2 tablespoons garlic powder
1/4 cup Worcestershire sauce
2 tablespoons monosodium glutamate
1 teaspoon hot pepper sauce

Directions

In a medium bowl, thoroughly mix the barbeque sauce, wine, onion powder, garlic powder, Worcestershire sauce, meat tenderizer and hot pepper sauce.

Tangy BBQ Rub

Ingredients

1/2 cup instant orange drink mix
1 teaspoon cayenne pepper
1/2 teaspoon paprika
1 teaspoon garlic powder
1/2 teaspoon ground allspice
1/2 teaspoon onion salt

Directions

Mix together the instant orange drink mix, cayenne pepper, paprika, garlic powder, allspice, and onion salt. Store at room temperature in an airtight container until used. Rub into chicken or pork and grill as desired.

Carol's Spicy BBQ Sauce

Ingredients

1 tablespoon hot pepper sauce
1 tablespoon Worcestershire sauce
2 tablespoons steak sauce
1/4 teaspoon meat tenderizer
1/4 teaspoon onion powder
1/4 teaspoon crushed red pepper flakes
2 tablespoons minced garlic

Directions

In a small bowl, combine the hot pepper sauce, Worcestershire sauce, steak sauce, meat tenderizer, onion powder, crushed red pepper flakes and minced garlic. Mix together well and apply to your favorite meat.

Absolutely Awesome BBQ Sauce

Ingredients

1 cup brown sugar
1/2 cup chile sauce
1/2 cup rum
1/4 cup soy sauce
1/4 cup ketchup
1/4 cup Worcestershire sauce
2 cloves garlic, crushed
1 teaspoon ground dry mustard
ground black pepper to taste

Directions

In a saucepan over low heat, mix the brown sugar, chile sauce, rum, soy sauce, ketchup, Worcestershire sauce, garlic, dry mustard, and pepper. Simmer 30 minutes, stirring occasionally. Cool, and refrigerate until ready to use.

Texas Hickory BBQ Chicken

Ingredients

2 (12 fluid ounce) cans beer
2 cups hickory wood chips, or as much as you like
4 chicken leg quarters
2 cups barbeque sauce
salt and pepper to taste
heavy duty aluminum foil

Directions

Preheat an outdoor grill for medium heat. Coat the grill surface lightly with oil. Pour beer into a pan or bowl, and add wood chips. Let soak while the grill heats up.

When the coals are ready, sprinkle the hickory chips over them. Place chicken pieces on the grill, cover, and cook for 15 minutes. Turn over, cover and grill for an additional 15 minutes. Remove the chicken pieces from the grill, and place each leg quarter onto a large square of aluminum foil. Cover with barbeque sauce, and fold the foil into a packet around each piece of chicken.

Return chicken packets to the grill, and cook for an additional 15 minutes per side. Remove packets, and serve with more barbeque sauce.

White BBQ Sauce

Ingredients

2 cups mayonnaise
2 tablespoons ground black pepper
2 tablespoons salt
6 tablespoons lemon juice
6 tablespoons distilled white vinegar
4 tablespoons white sugar

Directions

In a medium bowl, combine the mayonnaise, pepper, salt, lemon juice, vinegar and sugar. Mix all together until smooth. Use to baste chicken, pork chops or ribs as they cook on the grill. Serve extra as dipping sauce!

Carolina BBQ Pork Sauce

Ingredients

2 cups distilled white vinegar
2/3 cup ketchup
1 cup water
1 tablespoon white sugar
salt and pepper to taste
1 teaspoon crushed red pepper
1 teaspoon red pepper flakes

Directions

In a sauce pan, combine vinegar, ketchup, water and sugar. Season with salt, black pepper, cayenne pepper and red pepper flakes. Bring to a boil, reduce heat and simmer until sugar is dissolved.

Big John's BBQ Ribs and Dry Spice Rub

Ingredients

1 cup chili powder
1 tablespoon dried minced garlic
1 teaspoon onion powder
1/2 teaspoon ground cumin
1 1/2 teaspoons salt
2 tablespoons seasoning salt
B
2 pounds rib roast
B
4 cups canned tomato sauce
1/4 cup packed brown sugar
1/2 cup chopped fresh tomato
1/4 tablespoon Worcestershire sauce
2 tablespoons dried onion flakes
1/4 cup soy sauce
1/4 cup water

Directions

In a small bowl or jar, mix together chile powder, dried minced garlic, onion powder, cumin, salt and seasoning salt.

Place rib roast on a medium baking sheet. Rub vigorously with 1/2 the chile powder mixture. Cover and refrigerate 4 to 6 hours.

In a medium saucepan, mix together 1/2 the chile powder mixture, tomato sauce, brown sugar, tomato, Worcestershire sauce, dried onion flakes, soy sauce and water. Cook 3 to 5 hours, stirring occasionally, over low heat.

Prepare an outdoor grill for indirect heat. Lightly oil grate.

Cook ribs covered on the prepared grill 3 to 5 hours, or to desired doneness. Brush with the sauce mixture from the medium saucepan during the last minutes of cooking. Serve with remaining sauce mixture.

Oven Baked BBQ Ribs

Ingredients

2 cups sliced onions
2 cups ketchup
2 cups water
4 teaspoons salt
1/4 cup Worcestershire sauce
1/2 cup white vinegar
1/2 cup dark brown sugar
4 teaspoons dry mustard
4 pounds pork spareribs

Directions

Preheat oven to 350 degrees F (175 degrees C).

In a large bowl, combine onions, ketchup, water, salt, Worcestershire sauce, vinegar and mustard. Split ribs down the center between the bones.

Heat a large lightly oiled skillet over medium-high heat. Add ribs and sear until browned. This may have to be done in several batches.

Place ribs in a single layer in two baking pans or casserole dishes. Pour half of the sauce over the ribs, reserve remainder.

Bake ribs in preheated oven for 3 hours. Turn and baste meat every twenty minutes with remaining sauce, using all sauce by two hours. Continue turning and basting ribs using sauce in the pan during the last hour of baking.

BBQ Fried Chicken

Ingredients

3 pounds skinless, boneless chicken breast halves - cut into 1 inch strips
3 cups all-purpose flour
2 teaspoons garlic pepper seasoning
2 cups buttermilk
3/4 cup honey barbecue sauce
2 eggs

Directions

Preheat the oven to 350 degrees F (175 degrees F). Spray a baking sheet with nonstick cooking spray.

In a shallow dish, stir together the flour and garlic pepper. In a separate bowl, whisk together the buttermilk, barbeque sauce, and eggs. Coat chicken with the flour mixture, then dip into the buttermilk mixture. Dip into the flour mixture again. Place chicken strips on the prepared baking sheet.

Bake for 30 minutes in the preheated oven, or until golden brown on one side. Turn over, and continue to cook until golden on the other side, 20 to 30 minutes.

BBQ Steak Teriyaki

Ingredients

1 1/2 pounds flank steak
10 fluid ounces teriyaki sauce
1 teaspoon ground ginger
1 tablespoon dark sesame oil
1 tablespoon grated orange zest
1/4 cup cider vinegar
1/4 cup water
1/8 teaspoon cayenne pepper
2 cloves garlic, minced

Directions

In a medium bowl, mix together teriyaki sauce, ginger, sesame oil, orange zest, vinegar, water, cayenne pepper, and garlic. Place steak in a shallow dish, and pour marinade over meat. Cover, and refrigerate for at least 2 hours.

Preheat grill for high heat.

Lightly oil the grate, and place meat on grill. Cook for 3 to 5 minutes per side. Test for doneness.

Korean BBQ Chicken Marinade

Ingredients

1 cup white sugar
1 cup soy sauce
1 cup water
1 teaspoon onion powder
1 teaspoon ground ginger
1 tablespoon lemon juice (optional)
4 teaspoons hot chile paste (optional)

Directions

In a medium saucepan over high heat, whisk together the sugar, soy sauce, water, onion powder, and ground ginger. Bring to a boil. Reduce heat to low, and simmer 5 minutes.

Remove the mixture from heat, cool, and whisk in lemon juice and hot chile paste. Place chicken in the mixture. Cover, and marinate in the refrigerator at least 4 hours before preparing chicken as desired.

BBQ Pork Sandwiches

Ingredients

6 pounds pork butt roast
garlic salt to taste
1 (18 ounce) bottle hickory flavored barbecue sauce
8 hamburger buns

Directions

Preheat oven to 350 degrees F (175 degrees C). Place roast in a 9x13 inch pan, sprinkle with garlic salt, and cover with foil.

Bake in preheated oven for 3 to 4 hours, or until a meat thermometer inserted reads 160 degrees F (70 degrees C.) Preheat an outdoor grill for high heat and lightly oil grate.

Grill roast for 10 minutes on each side. Return roast to the pan, and shred the meat using two forks. Stir in barbecue sauce, and return to the oven for 20 minutes, or until heated through. Spoon meat onto buns.

Spicy BBQ Chicken

Ingredients

2 tablespoons vegetable oil
1/4 cup onion, finely chopped
1 clove garlic, minced
3/4 cup ketchup
1/3 cup vinegar
1 tablespoon Worcestershire sauce
2 teaspoons brown sugar
1 teaspoon dry mustard
1/2 teaspoon salt
1/4 teaspoon black pepper
1/4 (5 ounce) bottle hot pepper sauce
1 (3 pound) chicken, cut into pieces

Directions

Heat the oil in a skillet over medium heat and cook the onion and garlic until tender. Mix in ketchup, vinegar, Worcestershire sauce, brown sugar, dry mustard, salt, pepper and hot sauce. Bring to a boil. Reduce heat to low and simmer 10 minutes, stirring occasionally. Remove from heat and set aside.

Preheat grill for high heat.

Lightly oil grill grate. Place chicken on grill. Brush constantly with the sauce and cook 8 to 15 minutes on each side, depending on size of piece, until juices run clear. Discard any remaining sauce.

Korean BBQ Galbi

Ingredients

5 pounds beef short ribs, cut flanken style
5 cloves garlic
1 onion, coarsely chopped
1 Asian pear, cored and cubed
1 cup soy sauce (such as KikkomanB®)
1 cup brown sugar
1/4 cup honey
1/4 cup sesame oil
black pepper to taste

Directions

Place the ribs in a large stockpot and cover with cold water. Soak ribs, refrigerated, for 1 hour to pull out any blood. Drain.

Combine garlic, onion, and Asian pear in a blender and puree. Pour into a large bowl and stir in the soy sauce, brown sugar, honey, sesame oil, and black pepper. Marinate ribs in the soy mixture, covered, overnight.

Preheat an outdoor grill for high heat, and lightly oil the grate.

Grill ribs until the meat is tender and the outside is crusty, 5 to 10 minutes per side.

Carolina BBQ Sauce

Ingredients

2 cups apple cider vinegar
1 1/2 cups apple cider
1 cup dark brown sugar
1 tablespoon yellow mustard seed
2 tablespoons Dijon mustard
1/2 cup tomato paste
1/4 teaspoon salt
1/4 teaspoon fresh ground black pepper
2 smoked pork neck bones

Directions

Combine the cider vinegar, apple cider, brown sugar, mustard seed, Dijon mustard, tomato paste, salt, black pepper, and neck bones in a heavy-bottomed saucepan over medium heat; simmer until the sauce thickens, 30 to 40 minutes. Skim any foam from the surface of the liquid and discard. Remove and discard the neck bones. Cool the sauce to room temperature or use immediately.

Slow Cooker BBQ Pork Chops

Ingredients

8 pork chops
1 (18 ounce) bottle barbecue sauce

Directions

Spread a thin layer of barbeque sauce on the bottom of a slow cooker. Alternately layer pork chops with barbeque sauce, pouring the remainder of the bottle over the top of the final layer of chops.

Cook on HIGH setting for 3 to 4 hours, or all day on LOW setting.

Uncle Pauly's Carolina BBQ Sauce

Ingredients

2 (32 ounce) bottles ketchup
1 tablespoon Worcestershire sauce
1 tablespoon hot pepper sauce
1 tablespoon chili powder
2 tablespoons paprika
3 tablespoons ground black pepper
3 tablespoons salt
3/4 teaspoon ground mustard

Directions

Whisk together the ketchup, Worcestershire sauce, and hot pepper sauce in a mixing bowl. Sprinkle in the chili powder, paprika, black pepper, salt, and mustard. Whisk until evenly blended. The barbeque sauce is ready to use immediately.

BBQ Sausage and Peppers

Ingredients

2 pounds spicy Italian sausage, sliced
1 large red bell pepper, cut into large chunks
1/4 pound jalapeno peppers, cut into large pieces
1 large red onion, cut into chunks
1 (12 fluid ounce) can beer
1/2 pound sliced provolone cheese

Directions

Place sausage, red bell pepper, jalapeno peppers, and red onion in a large bowl. Pour in beer. Cover, and marinate in the refrigerator at least 1 hour.

Preheat an outdoor grill for high heat, and lightly oil grate.

Alternately thread sausage, red pepper, jalapenos, and onion onto skewers. Cook on the prepared grill until sausage is evenly brown and vegetables are tender. Melt provolone cheese over the hot ingredients during the last few minutes of cooking.

BBQ Salmon over Mixed Greens

Ingredients

2 tablespoons chili powder
1 tablespoon garlic powder
1 tablespoon onion powder
3 tablespoons white sugar
1 tablespoon salt
1/2 teaspoon ground allspice
1/2 teaspoon ground cumin
1/4 teaspoon ground white pepper
1 tablespoon paprika
6 (6 ounce) fillets salmon
olive oil
1 1/2 cups tomato-vegetable juice cocktail
1 tablespoon balsamic or cider vinegar
1/2 cup chopped tomatoes
4 tablespoons olive oil
1 pound mixed salad greens, rinsed and dried

Directions

In a small bowl, mix together chili powder, garlic powder, onion powder, sugar, salt, allspice, cumin, white pepper, and paprika. Reserve 1 1/2 tablespoons of the mixture for the vinaigrette, and sprinkle remaining spice mixture over salmon fillets. Cover, and refrigerate for 6 hours.

Preheat grill for high heat.

Lightly oil grill grate, and spread a small amount of olive oil on salmon fillets. Cook salmon 4 to 5 minutes per side, or until easily flaked with a fork.

In a small bowl, mix together tomato-vegetable juice cocktail, vinegar, tomatoes, olive oil, and reserved spice mixture to make vinaigrette. Place salad greens in a large bowl, drizzle with vinaigrette, and toss to coat.

Divide greens among individual serving plates. Top each plate with a salmon fillet, and spoon any remaining vinaigrette over the salmon.

Canadian Barn BBQ Sauce

Ingredients

1/2 cup applesauce
1/2 cup ketchup
2 cups packed brown sugar
6 tablespoons lemon juice
1/2 teaspoon salt
1/2 teaspoon black pepper
1/2 teaspoon paprika
1/2 teaspoon garlic salt
1/2 teaspoon ground cinnamon

Directions

In a medium bowl, mix applesauce, ketchup, packed brown sugar, lemon juice, salt, black pepper, paprika, garlic salt and ground cinnamon. Use the mixture to marinate ribs in the refrigerator for at least 30 minutes before preparing as desired. Also use for basting the ribs while cooking.

BBQ Chicken Sandwiches

Ingredients

2 (4 pound) whole chickens, cut up
1 1/2 cups ketchup
3/4 cup prepared mustard
5 tablespoons brown sugar
5 tablespoons minced garlic
5 tablespoons honey
1/4 cup steak sauce
4 tablespoons lemon juice
3 tablespoons liquid smoke flavoring
salt and pepper to taste
8 hamburger buns
4 cups prepared coleslaw (optional)

Directions

Place chicken in a large pot with enough water to cover. Bring to a boil, and cook until chicken comes off the bone easily, about 3 hours. Make sauce while the chicken cooks.

In a saucepan over medium heat, mix together the ketchup, mustard, brown sugar, garlic, honey, steak sauce, lemon juice, and liquid smoke. Season with salt and pepper. Bring to a gentle boil, and simmer for about 10 minutes. Set aside to allow flavors to mingle.

When the chicken is done, remove all meat from the bones, and chop or shred into small pieces. Place in a pan with the sauce, and cook for about 15 minutes to let the flavor of the sauce soak into the chicken. Spoon barbequed chicken onto buns, and top with coleslaw if you like.

Carolina BBQ

Ingredients

6 pounds pork shoulder
1 bay leaf
1 teaspoon crushed red pepper flakes
4 cups water
1 cup vinegar
1/3 cup white sugar
3 tablespoons ketchup
1 tablespoon Worcestershire sauce
1 teaspoon dry mustard
1 clove garlic, pressed

Directions

Place pork shoulder, bay leaf, red pepper and water in large pot with lid. Bring to boil. Simmer covered 4 to 5 hours until meat is tender. Let meat cool in broth. Remove excess fat from broth and shred meat.

Take 3 cups of liquid and bring to boil. Combine liquid with vinegar, sugar, ketchup, Worcestershire sauce and garlic. Add shredded pork and salt. Heat through uncovered.

Bubba's Best BBQ Sauce

Ingredients

1 cup cola-flavored carbonated beverage
1 cup canned tomato sauce
1 (6 ounce) can tomato paste
1/4 cup butter
1/2 cup Worcestershire sauce
1/2 cup packed brown sugar
1/2 cup molasses
1/2 cup cider vinegar
2 1/2 teaspoons balsamic vinegar
1 1/2 tablespoons steak sauce
1 tablespoon yellow mustard
1 tablespoon chili powder
1 teaspoon dried savory
1 teaspoon onion powder
1 teaspoon garlic salt
1 teaspoon hot pepper sauce

Directions

In a large saucepan, mix together the cola, tomato sauce, tomato paste, butter, Worcestershire sauce, brown sugar, molasses, cider and balsamic vinegars, steak sauce, and mustard. Season with chili powder, savory, onion powder, garlic salt, and hot pepper sauce, and stir to blend. Cook over low heat, stirring occasionally, until the mixture is thick enough to coat the back of a metal spoon.

Slow Roasted BBQ Beef Roast

Ingredients

5 pounds boneless rump roast
2 cloves garlic, sliced
1 teaspoon Spanish paprika
1 teaspoon salt
1 teaspoon pepper
1/4 teaspoon dried rosemary
1/4 teaspoon dried thyme

Directions

Prepare an outdoor rotisserie grill for medium heat.

Cut slits on all sides of the roast, and insert garlic slices.

In a small bowl, mix paprika, salt, pepper, rosemary, and thyme. Rub the mixture over the roast.

Place roast on the prepared rotisserie, and cook 2 to 5 hours, to a minimum internal temperature of 145 degrees F (63 degrees C). Allow to rest about 20 minutes before slicing.

Kickin' BBQ Sauce

Ingredients

2 cups apple cider
1/2 cup balsamic vinegar
1 1/4 cups ketchup
1/2 cup honey mustard
1/2 cup prepared yellow mustard
1/2 cup coarsely ground mustard
1/3 cup honey
1/3 cup molasses
1/3 cup cane syrup
1 (12 ounce) bottle dark beer
1/2 cup brewed coffee
1/2 cup Worcestershire sauce
1/2 cup soy sauce
1/2 cup Louisiana-style hot sauce
1 teaspoon ground black pepper
1 teaspoon celery salt
1 habanero pepper, seeded and minced

Directions

Place the apple cider, balsamic vinegar, ketchup, honey mustard, yellow mustard, coarse mustard, honey, molasses, cane syrup, beer, coffee, Worcestershire sauce, soy sauce, hot sauce, black pepper, celery salt, and the habanero pepper in a large pan. Simmer the mixture over low heat until thoroughly blended, about 25 minutes. Remove from the stove, cool, pour into a covered container, and refrigerate until needed.

BBQ Chicken Pizza

Ingredients

1 (12 inch) pre-baked pizza crust
1 cup spicy barbeque sauce
2 skinless boneless chicken breast halves, cooked and cubed
1/2 cup chopped fresh cilantro
1 cup sliced pepperoncini peppers
1 cup chopped red onion
2 cups shredded Colby-Monterey Jack cheese

Directions

Preheat oven to 350 degrees F (175 degrees C).

Place pizza crust on a medium baking sheet. Spread the crust with barbeque sauce. Top with chicken, cilantro, pepperoncini peppers, onion, and cheese.

Bake in the preheated oven for 15 minutes, or until cheese is melted and bubbly.

Bob's BBQ Sauce

Ingredients

1/2 cup brown sugar
2 tablespoons cider vinegar
1/4 cup ketchup
1 teaspoon ground dry mustard
1 teaspoon Worcestershire sauce
1 teaspoon horseradish sauce

Directions

In a bowl, mix the brown sugar, cider vinegar, ketchup, dry mustard, Worcestershire sauce, and horseradish sauce. Refrigerate until ready to use.

North Carolina BBQ Sauce

Ingredients

1 gallon white vinegar
1 1/3 cups cayenne pepper
1 1/8 cups ground black pepper
3/4 cup mustard powder
1/2 cup salt
3 lemons
2 (10 fluid ounce) bottles Worcestershire sauce

Directions

Combine the vinegar, cayenne pepper, black pepper, mustard powder, salt, lemons, and Worcestershire sauce in a large pot; bring to a simmer. Bring to a boil, then turn heat to low and simmer for at least 30 minutes.

BBQ Pie

Ingredients

1 1/2 pounds ground beef
1/4 cup diced onion
1/4 teaspoon ground black pepper
2 (15 ounce) cans baked beans with pork
1 teaspoon Worcestershire sauce
1 cup barbeque sauce
1 cup biscuit baking mix
1/2 cup milk
1 egg
1/4 cup shredded Cheddar cheese
1 tablespoon barbecue sauce

Directions

Preheat the oven to 350 degrees F (175 degrees C).

Crumble the ground beef into a large skillet over medium heat. When it is starting to brown, stir in the onion and season with pepper. Continue to cook and stir until beef is browned and the onion is tender.

Drain off the grease from the beef, and stir in the baked beans, Worcestershire sauce and 1 cup of barbeque sauce. Transfer to a large casserole dish. In a separate bowl, mix together the baking mix, milk and egg. Pour this mixture evenly over the beef and beans in the dish.

Bake for 40 to 45 minutes in the preheated oven, until the biscuit toping is golden brown. Spread a small amount of barbeque sauce over the top and sprinkle with Cheddar cheese while hot from the oven.

BBQ Chicken Wings

Ingredients

1/2 cup teriyaki sauce
1 cup oyster sauce
1/4 cup soy sauce
1/4 cup ketchup
2 tablespoons garlic powder
1/4 cup gin
2 dashes liquid smoke flavoring
1/2 cup white sugar
1 1/2 pounds chicken wings, separated at joints, tips discarded
1/4 cup honey

Directions

In a large bowl, mix the teriyaki sauce, oyster sauce, soy sauce, ketchup, garlic powder, gin, liquid smoke, and sugar. Place the chicken wings in the bowl, cover, and marinate in the refrigerator 8 hours or overnight.

Preheat the grill for low heat.

Lightly oil the grill grate. Arrange chicken on the grill, and discard the marinade. Grill the chicken wings on one side for 20 minutes, then turn and brush with honey. Continue grilling 25 minutes, or until juices run clear.

Baked BBQ Fried Chicken

Ingredients

3 pounds skinless, boneless chicken breast halves - cut into strips
3 eggs
1 cup water
1/2 cup milk
2 tablespoons salt
2 tablespoons black pepper
6 cups all-purpose flour
1/4 cup salt
5 teaspoons black pepper
2 tablespoons minced garlic
2 tablespoons dry mesquite flavored seasoning mix
4 cups oil for frying, or as needed
1 teaspoon butter
1 (12 ounce) bottle barbecue sauce

Directions

In a large bowl, whisk together the eggs, water, milk, 2 tablespoons salt, and 2 tablespoons pepper with a fork until smooth. In another large bowl, stir together the flour, 1/4 cup salt, 5 teaspoons pepper, garlic, and mesquite seasoning.

Fill a large heavy skillet or wok halfway full with oil. Heat to 365 degrees F (180 degrees C). Use a fork to pick up one chicken strip at a time, and dip it into the egg mixture, then into the flour mixture, back into the egg mixture, and into the flour mixture again. Place coated strips into the hot oil to fry. Do not over crowd, just cook in batches. Once chicken is browned on one side, flip over, and brown on the other side.

Preheat the oven to 300 degrees F (150 degrees C). Butter one 12x20 inch glass baking dish, or two 9x13 inch baking dishes. Pour enough barbeque sauce into the dish to coat the bottom. Arrange fried chicken strips in rows in the prepared dish. Pour remaining sauce over the top.

Bake for 10 to 15 minutes in the preheated oven, until the sauce is caramelized onto the chicken.

BBQ Cola Meatballs

Ingredients

1 1/2 pounds lean ground beef
1 1/4 cups dry bread crumbs
1 egg
3 tablespoons grated onion
1 (1 ounce) package dry Ranch-style dressing mix

1 cup ketchup
2 tablespoons apple cider vinegar
3/4 cup cola-flavored carbonated beverage
1/2 cup chopped onion
1/2 cup chopped green bell pepper
1 teaspoon seasoning salt
1/2 teaspoon ground black pepper
1 tablespoon Worcestershire sauce

Directions

Preheat the oven to 375 degrees F (190 degrees C).

In a large bowl, mix together the ground beef, bread crumbs, egg, grated onion and Ranch dressing mix until well blended. Shape into 1 inch meatballs, and place on a 10x15 inch jellyroll pan, or any baking sheet with sides to catch the grease.

Bake for 30 minutes in the preheated oven, turning them over half way through. While the meatballs are roasting, mix together the ketchup, cider vinegar, cola, chopped onion and green pepper in a slow cooker. Season with seasoning salt, pepper, and Worcestershire sauce.

Remove meatballs from the baking sheet, and place into the sauce in the slow cooker. Cover and cook on Low for 3 hours, then remove the lid and cook for an additional 15 minutes before serving.

Slow Cooker BBQ Meatballs and Polish Sausage

Ingredients

1 (16 ounce) package kielbasa sausage
1 (16 ounce) jar salsa
1 (10 ounce) jar grape jelly
1 cup water
1 tablespoon lemon juice

2 eggs
1 small onion, chopped
2 pounds ground beef
1 teaspoon salt
1 teaspoon ground black pepper
1/2 cup cornflakes cereal, crushed

Directions

Fill a large pot with lightly-salted water and bring to a rolling boil over high heat. Stir in the kielbasa and return to a boil. Cook until hot, 8 to 10 minutes; drain and cut into bite sized pieces. Place the kielbasa into a slow cooker; stir in the salsa, grape jelly, water, and lemon juice.

Meanwhile, beat the eggs in a mixing bowl; mix in the onion, ground beef, salt, pepper, and crushed cornflakes. Mix with your hands until evenly incorporated. Roll the mixture into balls the size of a large walnut; place into the slow cooker.

Set the slow cooker on High and cook until the meatballs are no longer pink in the center, about 1 hour.

BBQ Bacon Ranch Dip

Ingredients

7 slices bacon
2 (8 ounce) packages cream cheese, softened
1 (1 ounce) envelope ranch dressing mix
1/2 cup barbeque sauce
1 green bell pepper, chopped
1 tomato, chopped
1 1/2 cups shredded sharp Cheddar cheese

Directions

Place the bacon in a large, deep skillet, and cook over medium-high heat, turning occasionally, until evenly browned, about 10 minutes. Drain the bacon slices on a paper towel-lined plate. Crumble the cooled bacon into a bowl and set aside.

Stir together the cream cheese and ranch dressing mix in a bowl until smooth. Spread the mixture on the bottom of a pie dish. Evenly spread the barbecue sauce on top of the cream cheese mixture. Layer the bacon, bell pepper, and tomato on top of the barbecue sauce and top with the Cheddar cheese. Cover and chill for 1 hour before serving.

Bulgogi (Korean BBQ)

Ingredients

1 cup soy sauce
1/2 cup pear juice or white wine
3 tablespoons white sugar
2 tablespoons chopped garlic
1 teaspoon sesame oil
1 teaspoon sesame seeds
1 tablespoon ground black pepper
1 teaspoon monosodium glutamate
1 (2 pound) beef rump roast, sliced into thin strips
1 onion, cut into thin strips

Directions

In a large bowl, mix together soy sauce, pear juice, sugar, garlic, sesame oil, sesame seeds, black pepper, and monosodium glutamate. Place beef and onions into the mixture, and stir to coat. Cover, and refrigerate for 1 hour.

Preheat grill pan over high heat. Brush oil over grill pan, and add beef and onions. Cook, turning to brown evenly, for 3 to 6 minutes, or until done.

Mustard Based BBQ Sauce

Ingredients

1 cup prepared yellow mustard
1/4 cup honey
1/4 cup light brown sugar
1/4 cup white vinegar
ground black pepper to taste

Directions

In a saucepan over medium heat, stir together the mustard, honey, brown sugar and vinegar. Season with black pepper. Bring to a boil, and let simmer for 5 minutes. Pour over cooked pulled pork or beef. If you want more flavor, let the meat simmer in the sauce for about 30 minutes.

Simple BBQ Ribs

Ingredients

2 1/2 pounds country style pork ribs
1 tablespoon garlic powder
1 teaspoon ground black pepper
2 tablespoons salt
1 cup barbeque sauce

Directions

Place ribs in a large pot with enough water to cover. Season with garlic powder, black pepper and salt. Bring water to a boil, and cook ribs until tender.

Preheat oven to 325 degrees F (165 degrees C).

Remove ribs from pot, and place them in a 9x13 inch baking dish. Pour barbeque sauce over ribs. Cover dish with aluminum foil, and bake in the preheated oven for 1 to 1 1/2 hours, or until internal temperature of pork has reached 160 degrees F (70 degrees C).

A Very Popular BBQ Sauce

Ingredients

1 1/2 cups brown sugar
1 1/2 cups ketchup
1/2 cup red wine vinegar
1/2 cup water
1 tablespoon Worcestershire sauce
2 1/2 tablespoons dry mustard
2 teaspoons paprika
2 teaspoons salt
1 1/2 teaspoons black pepper
2 dashes hot pepper sauce

Directions

In a blender, combine brown sugar, ketchup, vinegar, water and Worcestershire sauce. Season with mustard, paprika, salt, pepper, and hot pepper sauce. Blend until smooth.

Yoyo's BBQ Beans

Ingredients

1 pound ground beef
1 sweet onion, chopped
2 cloves garlic, minced
salt and ground black pepper to taste
1/2 teaspoon garlic powder
1/2 teaspoon onion powder
2 tablespoons dried parsley
1 (28 ounce) can baked beans with pork
1 1/2 tablespoons prepared yellow mustard
2 tablespoons brown sugar
2 tablespoons Worcestershire sauce
1 1/2 cups honey garlic barbecue sauce

Directions

Cook and stir the ground beef in a large skillet over medium-high heat until evenly browned; drain. Combine the onion and garlic in the skillet with the beef, and cook until the onion becomes transparent, 3 to 4 minutes. Stir the salt, pepper, garlic powder, onion powder, and parsley into the beef mixture; cook 1 to 2 minutes.

Stir the canned beans into the beef mixture. Add the mustard, brown sugar, Worcestershire sauce, and barbecue sauce and stir until blended. Taste and season with additional salt and pepper, if desired. Lower heat to medium-low and simmer mixture for 30 minutes to thoroughly combine flavors.

Real New Orleans Style BBQ Shrimp

Ingredients

5 pounds medium shrimp, with shells
2 pounds butter
1 medium sweet onion, minced
8 cloves garlic, minced
2 stalks celery, diced
1/4 cup chopped fresh parsley
2 tablespoons Creole seasoning
2 tablespoons dried rosemary
ground black pepper to taste
1/2 cup Worcestershire sauce
2 teaspoons fresh lemon juice

Directions

Preheat the oven to 350 degrees F (175 degrees C). Arrange the shrimp in a single layer in as many baking dishes as you need. Set aside.

Melt 1/2 cup of butter in a large skillet over medium heat. Add the onion, garlic, celery, parsley, Creole seasoning and rosemary. Cook and stir for a few minutes, until onion is tender. Add the rest of the butter and cook until melted over low heat. Stir in the pepper, Worcestershire sauce and lemon juice. Pour this mixture over the shrimp so that the shrimp are completely submerged.

Bake in the preheated oven until shrimp are pink, 15 to 20 minutes.

Ace's BBQ Sauce for Grilling

Ingredients

1 1/2 cups distilled white vinegar
3/4 cup prepared yellow mustard
1/4 cup margarine
2 teaspoons salt
1 teaspoon ground black pepper
2 teaspoons crushed red pepper flakes
1 clove garlic, minced
1 tablespoon white sugar

Directions

Stir the vinegar, mustard, margarine, salt, black pepper, red pepper flakes, garlic, and sugar together in a saucepan over medium-high heat until the mixture comes to a boil. Reduce heat to medium-low and simmer until thickened, about 25 minutes.

Chile Garlic BBQ Salmon

Ingredients

3 pounds whole salmon, cleaned
1/4 cup soy sauce
1 tablespoon chile sauce
1 tablespoon chopped fresh ginger root
1 clove garlic, chopped
1 lime, juiced
1 lime, zested
1 tablespoon brown sugar
3 green onions, chopped

Directions

Prepare outdoor grill for high heat.

Trim the tail and fins off of the salmon. Make several shallow cuts across the salmon's skin. Place salmon on 3 large, slightly overlapping sheets of aluminum foil.

In a bowl, stir together soy sauce, chile sauce, ginger, and garlic. Mix in lime juice, lime zest, and brown sugar. Spoon sauce over the salmon.

Fold the foil over the salmon, and crimp the edges to seal.

If using hot coals, move them to one side of the grill. Place the fish on the side of the grill that does not have coals directly underneath it, and close the lid. If using a gas grill, place the fish on one side, and turn off the flames directly underneath it; close the lid. Cook for 25 to 30 minutes. Remove to a serving platter, and pour any juices that may have collected in the foil over the top of the fish. Sprinkle with green onions.

Easiest BBQ Pork Chops

Ingredients

1 (10.75 ounce) can condensed cream of mushroom soup
1 cup ketchup
1 tablespoon Worcestershire sauce
1/2 cup chopped onion
6 pork chops

Directions

Combine soup, ketchup, Worcestershire sauce, and onions in slow cooker. Add pork chops.

Cover, and cook on Low for 6 hours.

Bill's Smoked BBQ Baby Back Ribs

Ingredients

5 pounds baby back pork ribs
1/2 gallon apple juice
1 head garlic, separated into cloves
1 tablespoon granulated garlic
2 cups barbeque sauce

Directions

Prepare charcoal in a smoker, and bring the temperature to 225 degrees F (110 degrees C).

Cut the ribs into smaller portions of 3 or 4 ribs, and place them in a large pot. Pour in enough apple juice to cover. Place a lid on the pot and bring to a boil. Remove from the heat, and let stand for 15 minutes.

Lightly oil the grate in your smoker. Place ribs on the grate, and throw a few cloves of garlic onto the hot coals. Close the smoker. Maintain the temperature at 225 degrees F (110 degrees C) by adding more charcoal as needed. Smoke the ribs for 7 hours, adding more garlic cloves to the coals occasionally.

Make a sauce by mixing together the barbeque sauce with 2 cups of the apple juice from the pot. Season with granulated garlic. Baste ribs with this sauce while continuing to cook for another 30 minutes.

BBQ Chicken Salad

Ingredients

2 skinless, boneless chicken breast halves
4 stalks celery, chopped
1 large red bell pepper, diced
1/2 red onion, diced
1 (8.75 ounce) can sweet corn, drained
1/4 cup barbeque sauce
2 tablespoons fat-free mayonnaise

Directions

Preheat grill for high heat.

Lightly oil grate. Grill chicken 10 minutes on each side, or until juices run clear. Remove from heat, cool, and cube.

In a large bowl, toss together the chicken, celery, red bell pepper, onion, and corn.

In a small bowl, mix together the barbeque sauce and mayonnaise. Pour over the chicken and veggies. Stir, and chill until ready to serve.

Caribbean BBQ Sauce

Ingredients

1 teaspoon vegetable oil
3 slices bacon, diced
1 medium onion, finely chopped
1 cup tomato sauce
1/2 cup black rum
1 lemon, juiced
1/3 cup brown sugar
1 dash chili sauce

Directions

Place vegetable oil, bacon, and onion in a medium skillet over medium high heat. Cook until bacon is evenly brown and onion is tender.

Stir tomato sauce and rum into the skillet with bacon and onion, and reduce heat. Simmer about 2 minutes. Mix in lemon juice, brown sugar, and chili sauce. Continue to simmer about 8 minutes.

Paul's Southern California BBQ Sauce

Ingredients

2 cups apple cider vinegar
1/4 cup ketchup
2 tablespoons finely chopped onion
1 clove garlic, peeled and minced
1 teaspoon dry mustard
1 teaspoon chili powder
1 teaspoon seasoning salt
1 teaspoon cayenne pepper
1 cup brown sugar

Directions

Place the apple cider vinegar in a medium saucepan, and bring to a boil. Mix in the ketchup, onion, garlic, dry mustard, chili powder, seasoning salt, and cayenne pepper. Stir in the brown sugar. Cook, stirring often, 10 to 15 minutes.

Reduce heat, and, stirring occasionally, allow the mixture to simmer about 45 minutes, until thickened. Cool before serving.

Pork BBQ

Ingredients

1 pound cubed beef stew meat
1 pound cubed pork loin
1 (10.75 ounce) can condensed tomato soup
1/4 cup Worcestershire sauce
1/2 cup vinegar
1 onion, diced
1 cup water

Directions

Preheat oven to 350 degrees F (175 degrees C).

Combine together in a baking dish: beef cubes, pork cubes, tomato soup, Worcestershire sauce, vinegar, onion and water. Bake in a preheated oven for 4 hours. Add more water if liquid evaporates. When done, remove from oven and shred with a wooden fork or a potato masher.

This and That BBQ Sauce

Ingredients

- 1/2 cup ketchup
- 1/2 cup brown sauce
- 6 tablespoons lemon juice
- 1/4 cup balsamic vinegar
- 1/4 cup white vinegar
- 1/4 cup Worcestershire sauce
- 2 tablespoons brown sugar
- 1/2 teaspoon dry mustard

Directions

In a medium saucepan over low heat, mix the ketchup, brown sauce, lemon juice, balsamic vinegar, white vinegar, and Worcestershire sauce. Blend in the brown sugar and dry mustard until dissolved. Simmer 10 minutes, until thickened. Remove from heat, and allow to cool before using on meats as desired.

BBQ Teriyaki Pork Kabobs

Ingredients

3 tablespoons soy sauce
3 tablespoons olive oil
1 clove garlic, minced
1/2 teaspoon crushed red pepper flakes
salt and pepper to taste
1 pound boneless pork loin, cut into 1 inch cubes
1 (14.5 ounce) can low-sodium beef broth
2 tablespoons cornstarch
2 tablespoons soy sauce
1 tablespoon brown sugar
2 cloves garlic, minced
1/4 teaspoon ground ginger
3 portobello mushrooms, cut into quarters
1 large red onion, cut into 12 wedges
12 cherry tomatoes
12 bite-size chunks fresh pineapple

Directions

In a shallow dish, mix together 3 tablespoons soy sauce, olive oil, 1 clove minced garlic, red pepper flakes, salt, and pepper. Add pork cubes, and turn to coat evenly with marinade. Cover, and refrigerate for 3 hours.

In a saucepan, combine beef broth, cornstarch, 2 tablespoons soy sauce, brown sugar, 2 cloves minced garlic, and ginger. Bring to a boil, stirring constantly. Reduce heat, and simmer 5 minutes.

Preheat an outdoor grill for high heat and lightly oil grate. Thread pork cubes onto skewers, alternating with mushrooms, onion, tomatoes, and pineapple chunks.

Cook on grill for 15 minutes, or until meat is cooked through. Turn skewers, and baste often with sauce during cooking.

Jack BBQ Sauce

Ingredients

1 cup ketchup
2 tablespoons steak sauce
1 teaspoon garlic salt
2 teaspoons liquid smoke flavoring
1 teaspoon onion powder
3 tablespoons brown sugar
2 teaspoons lemon juice
4 drops hot pepper sauce, or to taste
4 dashes Worcestershire sauce
2 tablespoons whiskey

Directions

In a saucepan combine ketchup, steak sauce, garlic salt, liquid smoke, onion powder and brown sugar. Add lemon juice, pepper sauce, Worcestershire sauce and whiskey. Warm over medium low heat until simmering.

Refrigerate for at least one hour before using, to let flavors mingle. Brush on meat during the last few minutes of grilling or baking.

Not recommended for marinating unless you omit the lemon juice, as the acid makes the chicken grainy.

BBQ Miso Chicken

Ingredients

1 cup miso paste
1 cup beer
1 cup low sodium soy sauce
1 cup white sugar
2 teaspoons sesame oil
1/8 teaspoon cayenne pepper
2 1/2 pounds skinless, boneless chicken breast halves

Directions

In a large bowl, combine the miso paste, beer, soy sauce, sugar, sesame oil, and cayenne pepper. Stir until the miso and sugar are completely dissolved. Set aside 1/2 cup of the sauce for basting during grilling. Submerge the chicken in the remaining marinade, cover bowl, and refrigerate for at least 2 hours.

Preheat grill for medium-high heat.

Lightly oil the grill grate. Remove the chicken from the marinade, and discard marinade. Grill chicken for 6 to 8 minutes per side, basting during the last few minutes with the reserved sauce. The chicken is done when it's juices run clear.

Easy BBQ Bake

Ingredients

3/4 cup barbecue sauce
3/4 cup honey
1/2 cup ketchup
1 onion, chopped
4 skinless, boneless chicken breast halves

Directions

Preheat oven to 400 degrees F (200 degrees C).

In a medium bowl, combine the barbecue sauce, honey, ketchup and onion and mix well. Place chicken in a 9x13 inch baking dish. Pour sauce over the chicken and cover dish with foil.

Bake at 400 degrees F (200 degrees C) for 45 minutes to 1 hour, or until chicken juices run clear.

Carolina BBQ Peppers

Ingredients

2 cups corn oil
2 cups cider vinegar
2 cups white sugar
4 cups ketchup
1 pound fresh jalapeno peppers, sliced into rings
1 pinch dried oregano
1 clove garlic, minced

Directions

In a large pot, stir together the corn oil, cider vinegar, sugar, and ketchup until sugar has dissolved completely. Bring to a boil, then add the jalapeno peppers. Reduce heat to low, and simmer for 10 minutes. Season with oregano and garlic.

Ladle into sterile pint jars, leaving 1/4 inch of space at the top. Wipe rims with a clean dry towel. Seal with lids and rings. Process in a hot water bath for 10 minutes to seal. Refrigerate any unsealed jars.

Best BBQ Rub in Texas

Ingredients

1 (16 ounce) bottle seasoning salt
1/4 cup paprika
2/3 cup chili powder
1 teaspoon ground ginger
1 teaspoon ground nutmeg
2 teaspoons ground dry mustard
1 teaspoon ground cloves
1 teaspoon dry mesquite flavored seasoning mix
2 tablespoons garlic salt
1 tablespoon black pepper
1 cup packed brown sugar

Directions

In a large bowl, mix seasoning salt, paprika, chili powder, ginger, nutmeg, dry mustard, cloves, dry mesquite flavored seasoning mix, garlic salt, black pepper and brown sugar.

Island BBQ Sauce

Ingredients

2 tablespoons olive oil
1 cup minced onion
2 cloves garlic, minced
3 (1 inch) pieces fresh ginger root, minced
2 cups ketchup
1/4 cup SPLENDA® Brown Sugar Blend
1/4 cup molasses
1/2 cup spiced rum, divided
3 tablespoons hoisin sauce
2 tablespoons tomato paste
2 tablespoons sherry vinegar
1 tablespoon chili powder
1/8 teaspoon cayenne pepper

Directions

Heat the olive oil in a saucepan over medium-high heat. Stir in the onion, garlic, and ginger, and cook until tender. Reduce heat to low. Mix in ketchup, SPLENDA® Brown Sugar Blend, molasses, rum, hoisin sauce, tomato paste, vinegar, chili powder, and cayenne pepper. Cook and stir 5 minutes, until well blended and heated through. Stir in remaining rum.

Slow Cooker BBQ Chicken

Ingredients

4 large skinless, boneless chicken breast halves
1 cup ketchup
2 tablespoons mustard
2 teaspoons lemon juice
1/4 teaspoon garlic powder
1/2 cup maple syrup
2 tablespoons Worcestershire sauce
1/2 teaspoon chili powder
1/8 teaspoon cayenne pepper
2 dashes hot pepper sauce, or to taste (optional)
8 sandwich rolls, split

Directions

Place the chicken breasts into the bottom of a slow cooker. In a bowl, stir together the ketchup, mustard, lemon juice, garlic powder, maple syrup, Worcestershire sauce, chili powder, cayenne pepper, and hot sauce until the mixture is well blended.

Pour the sauce over the chicken, set the cooker to Low, and cook for 6 hours. Shred the chicken with two forks, and cook for 30 more minutes. Serve the chicken and sauce spooned into the sandwich rolls.

Brisket with BBQ Sauce

Ingredients

4 pounds lean beef brisket
2 tablespoons liquid smoke flavoring
1 tablespoon onion salt
1 tablespoon garlic salt

1 1/2 tablespoons brown sugar
1 cup ketchup
3 tablespoons butter
1/4 cup water
1/2 teaspoon celery salt
1 tablespoon liquid smoke flavoring
2 tablespoons Worcestershire sauce
1 1/2 teaspoons mustard powder
salt and pepper to taste

Directions

Pour liquid smoke over brisket. Rub with onion salt and garlic salt. Roll brisket in foil and refrigerate overnight.

Preheat oven to 300 degrees F (150 degrees C). Place brisket in a large roasting pan. Cover and bake for 5 to 6 hours. Remove from oven, cool, and then slice. Put slices back into pan.

In a medium saucepan, combine brown sugar, ketchup, butter, water, celery salt, liquid smoke, Worcestershire sauce, mustard, salt and pepper. Stir, and cook until boiling.

Pour sauce over meat slices in pan. Cover and bake for 1 more hour.

Special Honey BBQ Sauce

Ingredients

2 cloves garlic, minced
1 tablespoon minced shallot
1/2 cup honey
2 cups barbecue sauce, your choice
3 tablespoons chopped fresh cilantro

Directions

In a medium, nonporous bowl, combine the garlic, shallot, honey, barbecue sauce and cilantro. Mix well and pour onto meat or poultry. Discard any leftover sauce.

# BBQ Tuna Fritters

Ingredients

1 (6 ounce) can light tuna in water, drained
1 egg
2/3 cup quick-cooking oats
3 tablespoons barbeque sauce
3 tablespoons chopped green onion
1/2 teaspoon hot pepper sauce, or to taste
1/2 teaspoon dried savory
1 pinch salt
2 tablespoons vegetable oil

Directions

In a medium bowl, stir together the tuna, egg and oats until blended. Mix in the barbeque sauce, green onion, hot pepper sauce, savory, and salt.

Heat the oil in a large skillet over medium heat. Spoon tablespoonfuls of the tuna mixture into the pan, and flatten slightly. Smaller patties hold together better. Cook until browned on each side, about 3 minutes per side.

BBQ Bill's Citrus Smoked Chicken

Ingredients

1 (6 pound) whole chicken
4 cups lemon-lime flavored carbonated beverage
1 tablespoon garlic powder
2 cups wood chips, soaked

Directions

Place the whole chicken into a large resealable plastic bag. Sprinkle in garlic powder, then pour in enough lemon-lime soda to cover the bird. Seal the bag, and place in the refrigerator overnight to marinate.

Light charcoal in an outdoor smoker, and wait until the temperature is at 225 degrees F (110 degrees C).

Remove chicken from the bag, and place on the grill grate. Discard marinade. Cover, and cook for 10 hours. Occasionally toss a handful of soaked wood chips on the coals.

Big E's BBQ Rub

Ingredients

1 tablespoon ground mustard
1 tablespoon seafood seasoning, such as Old Bay™
1 1/2 teaspoons garlic powder
1 tablespoon ground white pepper
1 tablespoon ground black pepper
1 tablespoon red pepper flakes
2 tablespoons paprika
1 tablespoon kosher salt
1 1/2 teaspoons ground cumin
3 tablespoons white sugar
3 tablespoons brown sugar

Directions

Mix together mustard, seafood seasoning, garlic powder, white pepper, black pepper, red pepper flakes, paprika, salt, cumin, white sugar, and brown sugar in a bowl until evenly combined.

To use, rub the mixture on up to 5 pounds of meat and refrigerate from 2 to 12 hours before smoking or grilling.

Oven BBQ Ribs

Ingredients

1 (12 fluid ounce) can or bottle beer
1 1/2 cups water
1 tablespoon salt
3 tablespoons vegetable oil
5 pounds pork spareribs

1 tablespoon butter
1 cup thinly sliced onions
2 cloves garlic, pressed
2 (8 ounce) cans diced tomatoes with juice
1 cup ketchup
3 tablespoons molasses
1 tablespoon Worcestershire sauce
1 tablespoon prepared mustard
1/4 teaspoon salt
1/2 tablespoon hot pepper sauce
1 tablespoon white vinegar
1/2 lemon, sliced into rounds

Directions

Pour beer and water into a large stock pot. Add salt and stir to dissolve. Bring mixture to a boil over medium high heat.

In a large skillet or frying pan, heat vegetable oil over high heat. Sear ribs on both sides. Place on paper towels to briefly drain. Add seared ribs to the beer/water mixture. Add more water as needed to cover the ribs. Cover pot and simmer for 2 hours.

While the ribs are simmering, melt the butter in a sauce pan and saute the onions and garlic until onions are translucent. Stir in tomatoes, ketchup, molasses, Worcestershire, mustard, salt, hot pepper sauce and vinegar. Bring to a slow boil, stirring constantly. Reduce heat to low and leave it simmering until the ribs are finished.

Preheat oven to 350 degrees F (175 degrees C).

Drain ribs and arrange them in a shallow roasting pan, or pans. Ladle the sauce over the ribs evenly, slice each slice of lemon in half, and distribute the half slices on top of the sauce. Cover with foil loosely, and place in the oven for 15 minutes, and then uncover for the last 10, a total of 25 minutes oven time. Remove rind from lemon slices, discard rind, returning lemon "meat" to sauce on top of the ribs, and serve ribs covering each with sauce on the plate.

Easy BBQ Flank Steak with Chipotle Mayo

Ingredients

Steak Marinade:
1/2 cup soy sauce
1/2 cup olive oil
4 1/2 tablespoons honey
6 cloves garlic, minced
3 tablespoons chopped fresh rosemary
1 1/2 tablespoons coarsely ground black pepper
1 teaspoon salt
2 pounds flank steak

Chipotle Mayo:
1 1/2 cups mayonnaise
1 (7 ounce) can chipotle peppers in adobo sauce

Directions

Combine soy sauce, olive oil, honey, garlic, rosemary, pepper, and salt in a resealable plastic bag. Add the steak, and turn to coat with the marinade; press out excess air, and seal the bag. Marinate in the refrigerator for 30 minutes, or overnight for better flavor.

Preheat an outdoor grill for medium-high heat. Discard marinade.

Lightly oil the grate. Grill the flank steak for 7 minutes per side, or to desired doneness. An instant-read thermometer inserted into the center should read 140 degrees F (60 degrees C). Let stand for 10 minutes before slicing very thinly against the grain.

Drain the chipotle peppers reserving 1 teaspoon of the adobo sauce. Finely chop the chipotle peppers. Stir together the mayonnaise, chipotle peppers, and reserved adobo sauce in a medium bowl. Serve the sauce with the steak.

Alaskan BBQ Salmon

Ingredients

1 cup brown sugar
1/2 cup honey
1 dash liquid smoke flavoring
1/2 cup apple cider vinegar
1 (4 pound) whole salmon fillet

Directions

Preheat grill for high heat.

In a small bowl, mix together brown sugar, honey, liquid smoke, and vinegar.

Brush one side of the salmon with the basting sauce. Place the salmon on the grill, basted side down. After about 7 minutes, generously baste the top, and turn over. Cook for about 8 more minutes, then brush on more basting sauce, turn, and cook for 2 minutes. Take care not to overcook the salmon as it will loose its juices and flavor if cooked too long.

Broth Marinated BBQ Steak

Ingredients

1 (10.5 ounce) can beef broth
1 (18 ounce) bottle barbeque sauce
2 (8 ounce) steaks beef tenderloin

Directions

Whisk together beef broth and barbeque sauce in a medium bowl.

Place beef tenderloin steaks in a medium bowl and cover with the beef broth and barbeque sauce mixture. Cover bowl and place in the refrigerator. Allow steaks to marinate a minimum of 2 hours (overnight is preferable).

Preheat an outdoor grill for high heat and lightly oil grate.

Grill steaks on the prepared grill for 7 to 8 minutes per side, or to desired doneness.

Easy BBQ Sauce

Ingredients

1 tablespoon olive oil
1 small onion, chopped
3 cloves garlic, crushed
1 fresh red chile pepper, finely chopped
1/4 cup dark brown sugar
1 teaspoon fennel seed, crushed
1 cup ketchup
2 tablespoons dark soy sauce
salt and pepper to taste

Directions

Heat the oil in a saucepan over medium heat. Stir in the onion, garlic, red chile pepper, brown sugar, and fennel seeds, and cook until onion is tender and sugar has melted. Mix in ketchup and soy sauce. Bring to a boil. Reduce heat to low, and simmer 10 minutes.

Easy and Simple Korean BBQ Ribs

Ingredients

1 cup soy sauce
1 cup white sugar
1 teaspoon ground black pepper
5 cloves garlic, chopped
3 green onions, chopped
2 tablespoons Asian (toasted) sesame oil
1 teaspoon sesame seeds
2 pounds Korean-style short ribs (beef chuck flanken, cut 1/3 to 1/2 inch thick across bones)

Directions

Whisk together the soy sauce and sugar in a bowl until the sugar has dissolved, and stir in the black pepper, garlic, green onions, sesame oil, and sesame seeds.

Place the ribs in a large bowl, and pour the marinade over the ribs. Stir to coat the ribs with the marinade, and refrigerate for 1 hour. Stir the ribs and marinade again, and refrigerate for 1 more hour.

Preheat an outdoor grill for medium-high heat, and lightly oil the grate.

Remove the ribs from the marinade, discard the marinade, and grill the ribs until brown and no longer pink in the center, about 5 minutes per side. Have a spray bottle of water handy in case the ribs flare up.

Honey Garlic BBQ Sauce

Ingredients

1 cube vegetable bouillon
1 cup boiling water
1/2 cup ketchup
2 tablespoons vegetarian Worcestershire sauce
1 teaspoon dry mustard
1 teaspoon dried minced onion flakes
1 1/2 teaspoons salt
1 tablespoon white sugar
1/8 teaspoon cayenne pepper, or to taste
2 tablespoons vegetable oil
1 slice lemon
1/4 cup honey
4 cloves garlic, minced

Directions

Dissolve vegetable bouillon in boiling water.

In a large saucepan over medium heat combine vegetable broth, ketchup, Worcestershire sauce, mustard, onion flakes, salt, sugar, cayenne pepper, oil, lemon, honey and garlic. Bring to a boil; reduce heat and simmer for 10 minutes.

Mike's BBQ Chili and Honey Lamb Marinade

Ingredients

2 cloves garlic, minced
1 tablespoon coarse-grain mustard
1 teaspoon grated lemon zest
2 tablespoons lemon juice
2 tablespoons honey
2 teaspoons curry powder
1 teaspoon Asian chile paste
1 teaspoon ground turmeric

Directions

In a glass bowl, stir together the garlic, mustard, lemon zest, lemon juice, honey, curry powder, chile paste and turmeric. Rub into any cut of lamb, and marinate for at least 3 hours before cooking as desired.

BBQ Chicken Calzones

Ingredients

4 slices bacon
1/2 small onion, chopped
3 cups shredded, cooked chicken breast meat
2/3 cup barbeque sauce
1 (10 ounce) can refrigerated pizza crust dough
1 cup shredded mozzarella cheese
2 tablespoons chopped fresh cilantro

Directions

Preheat the oven to 400 degrees F (200 degrees C).

Fry bacon in a large skillet over medium-high heat until crisp. Remove from the pan to drain on paper towels; crumble. Add the onion and shredded chicken to the hot bacon grease in the pan. Fry over medium heat until onion is tender. Stir in 1/3 cup of barbeque sauce, and remove from the heat. Mix in the cooked bacon.

Roll the pizza crust dough out onto a greased cookie sheet. Press out to an even thickness, and then cut in half. Divide the chicken mixture between the two pieces of dough, spreading on only half of each piece to within 1/2 inch of the edge. Drizzle the remaining sauce over the filling. Sprinkle the cheese and cilantro over the top. Fold the uncovered portion of dough over the filling, and press the edges together with a fork to seal.

Bake for 25 minutes in the preheated oven, or until browned to your liking. Cool for a few minutes, then cut each calzone in half. Each serving is half of a calzone. These can be served with additional barbeque sauce if you like.

Sarge's EZ Pulled Pork BBQ

Ingredients

1 (5 pound) pork butt roast
salt and pepper to taste
1 (14 ounce) can beef broth
1/4 cup brewed coffee

Directions

Cut roast in half. Rub each half with salt and pepper, and place in the slow cooker. Pour broth and coffee over the meat.

Turn the slow cooker to Low, and cover. Cook for 6 to 8 hours, or until the roast is fork tender.

Carefully remove the roast to a cutting board. Pull the meat off the bone with a fork. You may also chop it with a cleaver afterwards, if you like it really finely cut.

Pam's BBQ Flat Jacks

Ingredients

1 pound ground beef
1/4 cup chopped onion
1/2 cup barbeque sauce
1/2 teaspoon hot pepper sauce (e. g. Tabascoв„ў)
1 (7.5 ounce) package refrigerated biscuit dough
1 cup shredded Cheddar cheese

Directions

Preheat the oven to 375 degrees F (190 degrees C). Crumble the ground beef into a skillet over medium-high heat. As soon as it begins to brown a little, add the onion. Cook and stir until beef is evenly browned. Drain off grease, then stir in the barbeque sauce and hot pepper sauce. Set aside.

Peel the biscuits apart in round layers, and use them to line the bottom of a 9x13 inch baking dish. Spread the ground beef mixture over the biscuits, then top with shredded cheese.

Bake for 15 to 20 minutes in the preheated oven, until the biscuits are cooked through, and cheese is melted.

Slow Cooker BBQ Flat Iron Steak Sandwiches

Ingredients

1/2 cup ketchup
1/2 cup Italian dressing
2 tablespoons soy sauce
1 tablespoon molasses
2 pounds flat iron steak, cubed
1 tablespoon dried chopped onion
4 hoagie rolls, split lengthwise and toasted
1 cup prepared coleslaw (optional)

Directions

Mix the ketchup, Italian dressing, soy sauce, and molasses in a small bowl. Place the steak in slow cooker, sprinkle with onions, and pour the ketchup mixture over the steak.

Turn the slow cooker to High and cook for 1 hour. Reduce the heat to Low and continue cooking until the meat is tender, about 4 hours. Serve on hoagie buns and top with 1/4 cup coleslaw, if desired, for a southern bbq flavor.

BBQ Meatballs

Ingredients

1 (16 ounce) package frozen meatballs
1 (18 ounce) bottle barbecue sauce
1/4 cup ketchup

Directions

Place prepared meatballs, barbeque sauce, and ketchup in a slow cooker. Let cook on a low heat for 4 hours, stirring occasionally.

BBQ Corn

Ingredients

10 ears fresh corn with husks
1 quart beer
1 (7 pound) bag of ice cubes

Directions

Place whole ears of corn in an ice chest. Pour beer over top. Dump ice out over the ears of corn. Place the lid on the cooler, and let sit 8 hours, or overnight.

Preheat smoker to 250 degrees F (120 degrees C).

Place corn in the smoker and close the lid. Cook for 1 to 2 hours, turning every 20 minutes or so. Kernels should give easily under pressure when done. To eat, just peel back the husks and use them for a handle.

Best Carolina BBQ Meat Sauce

Ingredients

1 1/2 cups prepared yellow mustard
1/2 cup packed brown sugar
3/4 cup cider vinegar
3/4 cup beer
1 tablespoon chili powder
1 teaspoon freshly ground black pepper
1 teaspoon freshly ground white pepper
1/2 teaspoon cayenne pepper
1 1/2 teaspoons Worcestershire sauce
2 tablespoons butter, room temperature
1 1/2 teaspoons liquid smoke flavoring
1 teaspoon Louisiana-style hot sauce, or to taste

Directions

In a heavy non-reactive saucepan, stir together the mustard, brown sugar, vinegar, and beer. Season with chili powder and black, white, and cayenne peppers. Bring to a simmer over medium-low heat, and cook for about 20 minutes. DO NOT BOIL, or you will scorch the sugar and peppers.

Mix in the Worcestershire sauce, butter, and liquid smoke. Simmer for another 15 to 20 minutes. Taste, and season with hot sauce to your liking. Pour into an airtight jar, and refrigerate for overnight to allow flavors to blend. The vinegar taste may be a little strong until the sauce completely cools.

Quesadillas on the BBQ

Ingredients

1/2 cup salsa, divided
4 (10 inch) flour tortillas
1/4 cup chopped sweet onion
1/4 cup chopped green bell pepper
1/4 cup chopped red bell pepper
1/4 cup chopped tomato
2 tablespoons chopped fresh cilantro
2 tablespoons chopped fresh chives
1/4 cup sliced black olives
1 cup cooked and peeled shrimp
1/2 cup shredded Cheddar cheese
1/4 cup sour cream

Directions

Preheat an outdoor grill for low heat.

Spread 1 tablespoon of salsa on half of each tortilla. Distribute the onion, green bell pepper, red bell pepper, tomato, cilantro, chives, olives, and shrimp evenly among the tortillas. Sprinkle each with cheese, and fold tortillas in half to cover the filling.

Lightly oil the grill grate. Place the filled tortillas directly on the grill. Cook about 2 minutes per side, until cheese is melted and the tortilla has grill marks. Serve with remaining salsa and sour cream.

BBQ Pork for Sandwiches

Ingredients

1 (14 ounce) can beef broth
3 pounds boneless pork ribs
1 (18 ounce) bottle barbeque sauce

Directions

Pour can of beef broth into slow cooker, and add boneless pork ribs. Cook on High heat for 4 hours, or until meat shreds easily. Remove meat, and shred with two forks. It will seem that it's not working right away, but it will.

Preheat oven to 350 degrees F (175 degrees C). Transfer the shredded pork to a Dutch oven or iron skillet, and stir in barbeque sauce.

Bake in the preheated oven for 30 minutes, or until heated through.

Fruit BBQ Marinade

Ingredients

1 tablespoon olive oil
1 small onion, chopped
1/2 red bell pepper
1/4 cup brown sugar
1 teaspoon garlic
1 tablespoon dry mustard
1/2 cup cider vinegar
4 cups pineapple juice
1 (16 ounce) jar pineapple fruit preserves

Directions

Brown onions, and red peppers in olive oil. Add brown sugar, garlic, mustard, and cider vinegar. Cook for one minute on high or until bubbly. Add pineapple juice.

Marinade meat of choice overnight or up to 24 hours.

Cook on barbecue and baste frequently with the marinade. Near the end of the cooking, add preserves to top and allow to brown slightly.

BBQ Sauerkraut Casserole

Ingredients

1 1/2 pounds ground beef
1 small onion, chopped
1 (27 ounce) can sauerkraut, drained
2 cups tomato juice
1 cup brown sugar

Directions

Preheat an oven to 350 degrees F (175 degrees C).

Heat a large skillet over medium-high heat, and stir in the ground beef and onion. Cook until the beef is crumbly, evenly browned, and no longer pink. Drain, and discard any excess grease.

Pour the beef mixture into a 3-quart casserole dish. Layer the sauerkraut over the ground beef, pour the tomato juice over the sauerkraut, then sprinkle with brown sugar. Bake in the preheated oven until the sauce is bubbly, about 60 minutes.

Apple Radish BBQ Ribs

Ingredients

4 pounds pork spareribs
2 quarts apple juice
3 cups barbecue sauce
1/2 cup prepared horseradish
3 tablespoons Worcestershire sauce
1 teaspoon garlic salt

Directions

Place ribs in a stock pot, and cover with apple juice. Bring to a boil, reduce heat, and simmer for 1 to 2 hours. Preheat oven to 350 degrees F (175 degrees C).

In a medium bowl, mix together barbecue sauce, horseradish, Worcestershire sauce, and garlic salt. Stir in 3 tablespoons of the apple juice from the ribs.

Brush underside of ribs with 1/3 of the sauce. Turn them over, and place in roasting pan. Brush tops with remaining sauce.

Bake in preheated oven for 25 to 35 minutes, brushing occasionally with sauce.

Scalloped Potatoes for the BBQ

Ingredients

4 red potatoes, thinly sliced
1 large onion, chopped
4 cloves garlic, chopped
1/4 cup chopped fresh basil
1/4 cup butter, cubed
salt and pepper to taste

Directions

Preheat grill for medium heat.

Layer sliced potatoes on aluminum foil with the onion, garlic, basil, and butter. Season with salt and pepper. Fold foil around the potatoes to make a packet.

Place potato packet on heated grill over indirect heat, and cook for 30 minutes, or until potatoes are tender. Turn over packet halfway through cooking.

Reunion BBQ's

Ingredients

5 pounds ground beef
2 cups chopped onion
3 cups water
2 tablespoons ketchup
2 tablespoons chili powder
2 tablespoons salt
1 tablespoon pepper
1 teaspoon ground mustard
1 cup quick-cooking oats
24 hamburger buns, split

Directions

In a several large saucepans or Dutch ovens, brown beef and onion over medium heat; drain. Add water, ketchup, chili powder, salt, pepper and mustard; bring to a boil. Stir in oats. Reduce heat; cover and simmer for 30 minutes. Serve on buns.

Best Stovetop BBQ Ribs

Ingredients

1/4 cup steak sauce (such as A1B®)
1/4 cup ketchup
1 tablespoon Worcestershire sauce
1 tablespoon soy sauce
1 tablespoon minced garlic
1/4 cup water
4 (6 ounce) country style pork ribs
1 onion, cut into rings (optional)

Directions

Whisk together steak sauce, ketchup, Worcestershire sauce, soy sauce, garlic, and water in a bowl until smooth.

Place the pork ribs in a saucepan with a lid, and pour the sauce over the ribs. Spread raw onion rings over the ribs, and cover the pan. Bring to a boil over medium heat, and simmer the ribs in the sauce for 45 minutes, or until tender.

Jbird's Authentic Sweet Vinegar BBQ Sauce

Ingredients

3 cups apple cider vinegar
1/4 cup red pepper flakes
1/4 cup ground black pepper
1/2 cup salt
1/2 cup ketchup
1 cup honey

Directions

In a saucepan, stir together the vinegar, red pepper flakes, pepper and salt. Bring to a boil. Stir in the ketchup and honey; reduce heat to low, and simmer for 30 minutes.

BBQ Country Style Ribs

Ingredients

10 country style pork ribs
2 teaspoons minced garlic
1 lemon, thinly sliced
1 (18 ounce) bottle barbeque sauce

Directions

Preheat oven to 250 degrees F (120 degrees C).

In a shallow baking pan or roaster, place ribs in a single layer; salt if desired. Spread the garlic on the ribs, then place the lemon slices on top. Bake in a preheated oven for 2 hours - the ribs should be tender. Drain any grease and liquid. Pour BBQ sauce over the ribs. Return to oven and bake one more hour at 200 to 250 degrees F.

Grant's Famous Midnight Grill BBQ Sauce

Ingredients

1 (18 ounce) bottle barbeque sauce
2 tablespoons Scotch whiskey
1 1/2 teaspoons Worcestershire sauce
1/2 teaspoon ground ginger
1/2 teaspoon cayenne pepper
1/2 teaspoon paprika
1/2 teaspoon chili powder
1/2 teaspoon garlic powder
1/2 teaspoon onion salt
1/2 teaspoon dried oregano
1 tablespoon red pepper flakes
1 1/2 tablespoons white sugar
1/2 teaspoon ground black pepper, or to taste
1/4 teaspoon hot pepper sauce, or to taste

Directions

In a medium bowl, stir together the barbeque sauce, whiskey, Worcestershire sauce, ginger, cayenne pepper, paprika, chili powder, garlic powder, onion salt, oregano, red pepper flakes, sugar, ground black pepper, and hot pepper sauce. Cover, and keep refrigerated until ready to use.

BBQ Nachos

Ingredients

20 tortilla chips
1/4 pound smoked beef sausage
1/2 cup Cheddar cheese
1/4 cup barbeque sauce

Directions

Arrange the tortilla chips on a microwave-safe platter. Shred the sausage with a cheese grater; scatter evenly over the chips; top with Cheddar cheese. Drizzle the barbeque sauce over the nachos.

Heat in the microwave until the cheese melts, 15 to 30 seconds.

Krystal's Perfect Marinade for BBQ or Grilled

Ingredients

1/2 cup brown sugar
1/2 cup balsamic vinegar
1/2 cup soy sauce
1/4 cup olive oil
2 tablespoons Worcestershire sauce
2 tablespoons sesame oil
4 cloves garlic, chopped
1/2 teaspoon ground black pepper

Directions

Whisk together the brown sugar, vinegar, soy sauce, olive oil, Worcestershire sauce, sesame oil, garlic, and pepper until the sugar has dissolved.

BBQ Sauce to Live For

Ingredients

1 cup barbeque sauce
1 cup duck sauce

Directions

In a medium bowl, blend barbeque sauce and duck sauce. Chill in the refrigerator until serving.

Slow Cooker Wieners in Wiener BBQ Sauce

Ingredients

2 pounds hot dogs
1 (18 ounce) jar grape jelly
1 (8 ounce) jar prepared mustard
1 tablespoon brown sugar
1 tablespoon apple cider vinegar

Directions

Place the wieners in a slow cooker. In a medium bowl, combine the grape jelly, mustard, brown sugar and cider vinegar. Mix well and pour over the wieners.

Cook on low setting for at least 1 hour before serving.

Texas BBQ Beef Brisket

Ingredients

1 (3 pound) boneless beef brisket, flat cut
3/4 cup barbeque sauce
1/2 cup dry red wine

Rub:
2 tablespoons chili powder
1 tablespoon packed brown sugar
1 1/2 teaspoons garlic powder

Directions

Combine rub ingredients in small bowl; press evenly onto beef brisket. Place brisket, fat side up, in stockpot.

Combine barbecue sauce and wine in small bowl. Pour around brisket; bring to a boil. Reduce heat; cover tightly and simmer 2-1/2 to 3 hours or until brisket is fork-tender. Remove brisket; keep warm.

Skim fat from cooking liquid. Bring cooking liquid to a boil. Reduce heat to medium and cook, uncovered, 8 to 10 minutes or until reduced to 1 cup sauce, stirring occasionally.

Trim fat from brisket. Carve diagonally across the grain into thin slices. Serve with sauce.

BBQ NY Strip

Ingredients

1/2 cup extra virgin olive oil
1/2 cup Worcestershire sauce
1/4 cup minced garlic
1/4 cup steak seasoning
1 tablespoon red wine vinegar
1/2 teaspoon dried basil
1/2 teaspoon Italian seasoning
4 (1/2 pound) New York strip steaks

Directions

In a bowl, mix the olive oil, Worcestershire sauce, garlic, steak seasoning, red wine vinegar, basil, and Italian seasoning. Pour into a large resealable plastic bag. Pierce steaks on all sides with a fork, and place in the bag. Gently shake to coat. Seal bag and marinate steaks a minimum of 2 hours in the refrigerator.

Preheat grill for high heat.

Lightly oil the grill grate. Discard marinade. Place steaks on the grill, and cook 7 minutes on each side, or to desired doneness.

BBQ Steak

Ingredients

1 small onion, chopped
7 cloves garlic
1/2 cup olive oil
1/2 cup vinegar
1/2 cup soy sauce
2 tablespoons chopped fresh rosemary
2 tablespoons Dijon-style prepared mustard
2 teaspoons salt
1 teaspoon black pepper
1 (2 pound) tri-tip steak

Directions

Place onion, garlic, olive oil, vinegar, soy sauce, rosemary, mustard, salt, and pepper into the bowl of a food processor. Process until smooth. Place steak in a large resealable plastic bag. Pour marinade over steaks, seal, and refrigerate for about 3 hours.

Preheat the grill for high heat.

Brush grill grate with oil. Discard marinade, and place steak on the prepared grill. Cook for 7 minutes per side, or to desired doneness.

BBQ Pork Salad with Summer Fruits and Honey

Ingredients

4 cooked pork chops, sliced
8 cups mixed greens
2 nectarines, cut into 12-wedges each
1 grapefruit, segmented
2 avocados, cut into wedges
16 cherry tomatoes
1 tablespoon salad oil
2 tablespoons slivered, toasted almonds
salt and black pepper

Honey Balsamic Vinaigrette:
2 tablespoons balsamic vinegar
2 tablespoons honey
1/2 tablespoon Dijon mustard
2 tablespoons mayonnaise
1 teaspoon chili powder
1 teaspoon salt
1/2 teaspoon black pepper
3/8 cup salad oil

Directions

For the Vinaigrette: In a blender, combine all ingredients except oil. Blend at medium speed for one minute. Next, with blender at medium speed, pour oil very slowly into blender. Add salt and pepper.

For each serving, toss 2 cups greens with 2 tablespoons dressing, top with 4 cherry tomatoes, 1 sliced pork chop, 1/2 avocado, sliced in wedges, 1/2 nectarine sliced in wedges, 1/4 grapefruit segments. Drizzle with more dressing and sprinkle with toasted almonds. Serve immediately.

BBQ Sauce

Ingredients

2 tablespoons olive oil
1/4 cup minced sweet onion
3 cloves garlic, crushed
1 (8 ounce) can tomato sauce
1 (6 ounce) can tomato paste
1/4 cup cider vinegar
1/3 cup tomato juice
1 tablespoon Worcestershire sauce
1/2 teaspoon dry mustard
1/2 teaspoon cayenne
1/2 teaspoon paprika
1/3 cup Stevia Extract In The Raw® Cup For Cup
Fresh ground black pepper to taste

Directions

In medium saucepan cook minced onion and garlic in olive oil until onions turn opaque. Stir in remaining ingredients; blend well and simmer covered for 20 minutes.

BBQ Chili Pasta

Ingredients

1 (8 ounce) package rotini pasta
1 tablespoon olive oil
1 onion, chopped
8 ounces ground turkey
1 green bell pepper, chopped
1 (15 ounce) can whole kernel corn, drained
1 tablespoon chili powder
1 tablespoon dried oregano
1/2 teaspoon salt
1 (8 ounce) can tomato sauce
3/4 cup barbecue sauce

Directions

In a large pot with boiling salted water cook rotelle pasta until al dente. Drain.

Meanwhile, in a large non-stick skillet heat oil over medium-high heat, add onion and cook until onion for 2 minutes, or until softened. Add ground turkey and cook until no pink remains, about 3 to 4 minutes. Stir in chopped green bell pepper, corn, chili powder, dried oregano, salt, tomato sauce, and BBQ sauce. Bring mixture to a boil. Reduce heat to medium and simmer until slightly thickened, about 3 to 4 minutes, stirring occasionally.

In a large serving bowl, combine the turkey mixture with the pasta. Serve immediately.

Old Style BBQ Sauce

Ingredients

1 (28 ounce) bottle ketchup
1 (12 fluid ounce) can beer
1 small onion, diced
1 1/2 cups dark brown sugar
1/2 cup prepared mustard
3 tablespoons barbeque seasoning
2 tablespoons distilled white vinegar
1 teaspoon black pepper
1 teaspoon garlic powder

Directions

In a slow cooker, combine ketchup, beer, onion, brown sugar, mustard, barbecue seasoning, vinegar, pepper, and garlic powder. Simmer on low setting for 12 hours or overnight.

Dave's BBQ Sauce

Ingredients

2 cups ketchup
2 tablespoons brown sugar
1 tablespoon Worcestershire sauce
1 tablespoon soy sauce
1/2 teaspoon hot pepper sauce
1 lemon, juiced
1 small onion, finely chopped
1/2 teaspoon garlic powder
salt and pepper to taste

Directions

In a small bowl combine ketchup, brown sugar, Worcestershire sauce, soy sauce, hot sauce and lemon juice. Add the finely chopped onion, season with garlic powder, salt and pepper. Mix well.

Apply to meat around 5 minutes before you remove meat from the barbecue.

BBQ Chicken Pizza II

Ingredients

1 (12 inch) pre-baked pizza crust
1/2 cup barbecue sauce
1/2 cup diced grilled chicken
1/4 cup chopped red bell pepper
1/4 cup chopped green bell pepper
1/4 cup chopped red onion
1 cup shredded Monterey Jack cheese

Directions

Preheat oven to 450 degrees F (230 degrees C).

Place pizza crust on cookie sheet. Spread with barbecue sauce. Scatter chicken over top. Sprinkle evenly with red pepper, green pepper and onion. Cover with cheese.

Bake in preheated oven for 10 to 12 minutes, or until cheese is melted.

BBQ Quesadilla

Ingredients

1 (1 pound) package Bob Evans® Zesty Hot Sausage
1/2 cup thinly sliced red onion
1/2 cup Bob Evans® Wildfire BBQ Sauce
4 (10 inch) flour tortillas
1 cup shredded Monterey Jack cheese
Sour cream
Salsa

Directions

In skillet over medium heat crumble and cook sausage and onions until brown. Stir in BBQ sauce. Lay 2 of the tortillas on a flat surface. Top each with 1/4 cup cheese. Divide sausage mixture between the two. Sprinkle each with 1/4 cup cheese. Top with remaining tortillas. Heat large skillet over medium heat. Add a small amount of oil to coat bottom of skillet. Cook one quesadilla at a time until golden brown on each side, about 2 to 3 minutes per side. Cut into wedges and serve with sour cream and salsa.

BBQ Pork Pizza

Ingredients

1 (13.8 ounce) package refrigerated pizza dough
1 (18 ounce) container barbequed pulled pork
1/4 red onion, thinly sliced
1/2 cup dill pickle slices
2 cups shredded mozzarella cheese

Directions

Preheat oven to 425 degrees F (220 degrees C). Grease a 9x13 inch baking pan.

Roll the dough out into the prepared pan. Top the dough with the barbecued pork. Sprinkle with the red onions, and layer on the dill pickle slices. Sprinkle mozzarella cheese evenly over the top.

Bake in the preheated oven until crust is golden and cheese is melted, about 18 minutes.

Sweet Onion BBQ Burgers

Ingredients

1/2 cup dry bread crumbs
2 teaspoons onion salt
2 teaspoons brown sugar
1 egg, beaten
1 pound ground beef
1 1/4 cups barbecue sauce
SAUCE:
1/2 cup mayonnaise
1/2 cup barbecue sauce
1 teaspoon brown sugar
ONION TOPPING:
2 tablespoons butter
1/4 cup honey
2 large sweet onions, thinly sliced
4 slices smoked Cheddar cheese
4 hamburger buns, split

Directions

In a bowl, combine the bread crumbs, onion salt and brown sugar. Add egg. Crumble beef over mixture and mix well. Shape into four patties. Place in a shallow dish; pour barbecue sauce over patties. Cover and refrigerate for 2-4 hours.

In a small bowl, combine the sauce ingredients; cover and refrigerate until serving. For topping, melt butter in a large skillet. Stir in honey until blended. Add onions; saute for 15-20 minutes or until tender and lightly browned. Keep warm.

Drain and discard barbecue sauce. Grill patties, uncovered, over medium-hot heat for 5-7 minutes on each side or until juices run clear. Top each with a cheese slice; grill 1 minute longer or until cheese is melted. Serve on buns with sauce and onion topping.

Delayed Heat BBQ Sauce

Ingredients

3 tablespoons ground dry mustard
3 tablespoons water
1 cup dark brown sugar
3/4 cup cider vinegar
1/4 cup soy sauce
3 tablespoons chili powder
1 1/2 tablespoons ground black pepper

Directions

In a medium resealable container, blend ground dry mustard and water. Mix in dark brown sugar, cider vinegar, soy sauce, chili powder, and ground black pepper. Seal container, and shake until thoroughly blended.

BBQ Sauce

Ingredients

1/4 cup cider vinegar
1/2 cup ketchup
1/2 cup water
3 tablespoons white sugar
1 teaspoon salt
1 teaspoon chili powder

Directions

In a medium bowl or bottle, combine the vinegar, ketchup, water, sugar, salt and chili powder. Mix well and store in the refrigerator until ready for use.

BBQ Chicken Sandwiches

Ingredients

2 (4 pound) whole chickens, cut up
1 1/2 cups ketchup
3/4 cup prepared mustard
5 tablespoons brown sugar
5 tablespoons minced garlic
5 tablespoons honey
1/4 cup steak sauce
4 tablespoons lemon juice
3 tablespoons liquid smoke flavoring
salt and pepper to taste
8 hamburger buns
4 cups prepared coleslaw (optional)

Directions

Place chicken in a large pot with enough water to cover. Bring to a boil, and cook until chicken comes off the bone easily, about 3 hours. Make sauce while the chicken cooks.

In a saucepan over medium heat, mix together the ketchup, mustard, brown sugar, garlic, honey, steak sauce, lemon juice, and liquid smoke. Season with salt and pepper. Bring to a gentle boil, and simmer for about 10 minutes. Set aside to allow flavors to mingle.

When the chicken is done, remove all meat from the bones, and chop or shred into small pieces. Place in a pan with the sauce, and cook for about 15 minutes to let the flavor of the sauce soak into the chicken. Spoon barbequed chicken onto buns, and top with coleslaw if you like.

Dad's BBQ Roast

Ingredients

1 1/3 cups yellow mustard
2 (1 ounce) envelopes dry onion soup mix
1 (5 pound) beef rump roast

Directions

In a small bowl, mix together the mustard and onion soup mix. Lay out two long sheets of aluminum foil crosswise. Pat the roast dry, and place in the center of the foil. Generously coat the roast with the mustard mixture. Wrap the foil tightly around the roast, then apply one more piece of foil to really seal it in so that the roast can be rotated without all of the juices spilling out. This process may be done as early as the morning before.

Prepare an outdoor grill for indirect heat. For charcoal, light the coals, then move to one side of the grill. For gas, light only one burner, and cook on the unlit side.

Place the roast on the grill, and cover. Cook for about 2 hours, turning every 30 to 45 minutes, or until the internal temperature is at least 145 degrees F (63 degrees C).

Let stand for about 10 minutes before carving. Place on a deep serving plate before unwrapping so you can be sure to save the juices and mustard rub to slather on the beef slices.

BBQ Sauce for Cheaters

Ingredients

2 (18 ounce) bottles barbeque sauce
2 (10 ounce) cans diced tomatoes with green chile peppers, drained
2 1/2 tablespoons dark molasses

Directions

In a large saucepan over medium heat, whisk together barbeque sauce, diced tomatoes with green chile peppers and dark molasses. Simmer 30 minutes partially covered, stirring occasionally, until mixture has thickened.

Micky's Sticky Licky Sweet n Zesty BBQ Sauce

Ingredients

2 tablespoons butter
1/8 cup chopped onion
1/2 cup chopped celery
2 teaspoons minced garlic
1 cup ketchup
1/4 cup lemon juice
2 tablespoons white sugar
2 tablespoons white vinegar
1 tablespoon Worcestershire sauce
1 teaspoon dry mustard
1/2 teaspoon ground black pepper

Directions

Melt butter in a large skillet over medium heat. Saute onion, celery and garlic until soft and translucent. Stir in ketchup, lemon juice, sugar, vinegar, Worcestershire sauce, mustard and pepper. Simmer 15 to 20 minutes.

Tina's Best BBQ Lime Chicken

Ingredients

1 (4 pound) chicken, cut into pieces
2 teaspoons seasoning salt
2 teaspoons ground black pepper
1/2 teaspoon cayenne pepper
1 1/2 cups fresh lime juice
1 cup olive oil
8 cloves garlic, minced
1/2 cup chopped fresh cilantro

Directions

Wash chicken parts. Pat dry thoroughly. Pierce all pieces with a fork. In a small bowl, combine the seasoning salt, ground black pepper and cayenne pepper. Rub all chicken parts with the spices, then place the chicken into a large, resealable plastic bag.

In a separate medium bowl, combine the lime juice, olive oil, garlic and cilantro. Mix well and pour into the bag with the chicken. Seal and let marinate in the refrigerator for at least 2 hours.

Preheat an outdoor grill for low heat and lightly oil grate.

Remove chicken from the refrigerator and pour marinade into a small saucepan over medium high heat. Bring to a boil for about 1 to 2 minutes.

Grill chicken for about 1 1/2 hours. Brush with the marinade every 15 minutes. Chicken is done when juices run clear.

Grandpa Crotts BBQ Sauce

Ingredients

1/4 cup vegetable oil
1 1/2 cups ketchup
1 onion, chopped
1/4 cup fresh lemon juice
2 tablespoons prepared mustard
1/8 teaspoon hot pepper sauce
1/4 cup Worcestershire sauce

Directions

Place the oil, ketchup, onion, lemon juice, mustard, hot pepper sauce and Worcestershire sauce in a medium saucepan over low heat. Mix well and allow to simmer for 30 minutes.

BBQ Chuck Roast

Ingredients

1 (5 pound) chuck roast
1 cup barbeque sauce
1 cup teriyaki sauce
1 (12 fluid ounce) can or bottle beer
3 teaspoons minced garlic
3 teaspoons thinly sliced fresh ginger root
1 onion, finely chopped
3 teaspoons coarsely ground black pepper
2 teaspoons salt

Directions

In a large bowl, mix barbeque sauce, teriyaki sauce, beer, garlic, ginger, onion, black pepper, and salt. Place the roast into the marinade, cover and refrigerate for six hours, turning often.

Preheat an outdoor grill for indirect heat. Remove the roast from the marinade, and pour the marinade into a saucepan. Bring to a boil, and cook for 5 minutes. Set aside for use as a basting sauce.

Thread the roast onto a rotating barbecue spit above indirect heat. Cook the roast for two hours, or until the internal temperature of the roast is at least 145 degrees F (63 degrees C). Baste often during the last hour with reserved marinade.

Memorial Day Best BBQ Chicken Ever!

Ingredients

1/2 cup Worcestershire sauce
1 teaspoon Cajun seasoning
1 teaspoon garlic powder
2 1/2 tablespoons brown sugar
1 1/2 tablespoons ketchup
6 skinless, boneless chicken breast halves

Directions

In a large bowl, blend the Worcestershire sauce, Cajun seasoning, garlic powder, brown sugar, and ketchup. Place the chicken in the bowl, and coat thoroughly with the sauce mixture. Cover, and refrigerate 8 hours or overnight.

Heat an outdoor grill for medium heat, and lightly oil grate.

Discard the marinade, and grill chicken 6 to 8 minutes per side on the prepared grill, or until no longer pink and juices run clear.

Jim Goode's BBQ Beef Rub

Ingredients

2 1/2 tablespoons dark brown sugar
2 tablespoons paprika
2 teaspoons mustard powder
2 teaspoons onion powder
2 teaspoons garlic powder
1 1/2 teaspoons dried basil
1 teaspoon ground bay leaves
3/4 teaspoon ground coriander seed
3/4 teaspoon ground savory
3/4 teaspoon dried thyme
3/4 teaspoon ground black pepper
3/4 teaspoon ground white pepper
1/8 teaspoon ground cumin
salt to taste

Directions

In a small bowl, mix together the brown sugar, paprika, mustard powder, onion powder, garlic powder, basil, bay leaves, coriander, savory, thyme, black pepper, white pepper, cumin, and salt. Store in an airtight jar at room temperature until ready to use.

Buzzsaw's BBQ Sauce

Ingredients

1 teaspoon vegetable oil
1/2 onion, diced
1 clove garlic, minced
3 tablespoons Worcestershire sauce
3 tablespoons vinegar
2 tablespoons molasses
1 teaspoon prepared mustard
1 cup ketchup
1/2 cup cold water
1 teaspoon cornstarch

Directions

Heat the oil in a saucepan over medium heat, and saute the onion until tender and golden brown. Stir in garlic. Mix in Worcestershire sauce, vinegar, molasses, and mustard. Cook and stir 5 minutes, then mix in ketchup, cold water, and cornstarch. Reduce heat to low, and continue cooking 10 minutes, until thickened.

Blackberry BBQ Sauce

Ingredients

1/2 cup blackberry preserves
1 1/2 cups ketchup
1/8 cup brown sugar
1/8 teaspoon cayenne pepper
1/4 teaspoon mustard powder
2 tablespoons red wine vinegar

Directions

In a medium bowl, mix together blackberry preserves, ketchup, brown sugar, cayenne pepper, mustard powder, and red wine vinegar. Use to baste pork or beef ribs while grilling.

Kafta (BBQ)

Ingredients

1 1/2 pounds lean ground beef
1 medium onion, grated
1/2 cup finely chopped fresh parsley
1/4 teaspoon cayenne pepper
1/4 teaspoon ground allspice
1 teaspoon salt, or to taste
1/4 teaspoon black pepper
6 wooden or metal skewers

Directions

Preheat an outdoor grill for high heat. If using wooden skewers, soak in water.

In a large bowl, mix together the ground beef, onion, parsley, cayenne, allspice, salt and pepper until evenly blended. Divide into 6 portions, and press around one end of the skewers to form a log shape approximately 1 inch thick and 6 inches long.

Grill for 10 to 15 minutes, turning occasionally, until meat is no longer pink.

Ainaa's BBQ Chicken

Ingredients

1 (4 pound) chicken, cut into pieces
1/2 (10.75 ounce) can condensed tomato soup
1 tablespoon garlic powder
3 tablespoons ginger juice
1 teaspoon ground cardamom
1/2 tablespoon curry powder
1 teaspoon salt
1 teaspoon brown sugar
2 tablespoons lemon juice
1/2 cup buttermilk

Directions

FOR MARINADE: In a large bowl combine the soup, garlic powder, ginger juice, cardamom, curry powder, salt, brown sugar and lemon juice. Mix well. Marinate the chicken in the refrigerator overnight.

The next day, mix in the buttermilk, then grill the chicken until cooked through. You'll love it!

Thai Style BBQ Chicken

Ingredients

3 cloves garlic, minced
2 tablespoons minced fresh ginger root
1 lime, zested and juiced
1/4 teaspoon crushed red pepper flakes
1/2 cup water
1/4 cup soy sauce
1/4 cup Worcestershire sauce
1 tablespoon white sugar
6 skinless, boneless chicken breast halves

Directions

In a medium nonporous bowl, combine the garlic, ginger, lime zest, lime juice, crushed red pepper flakes, water, soy sauce, Worcestershire sauce and sugar. Mix well and place the chicken in the sauce, turning several times to coat. Cover and marinate in the refrigerator for 4 to 24 hours.

Preheat an outdoor grill for high heat and lightly oil grate.

Grill chicken over high heat for 6 to 8 minutes per side, or until internal temperature reaches 180 degrees F (80 degrees C). Discard any remaining marinade.

Korean BBQ Beef (Pul-Kogi)

Ingredients

1 pound beef top sirloin, thinly sliced
6 cloves garlic, minced
1/2 pear - peeled, cored, and minced
2 green onions, thinly sliced
4 tablespoons soy sauce
2 tablespoons white sugar
1 tablespoon sesame oil
1 tablespoon rice wine
1 tablespoon sesame seeds
1 teaspoon minced fresh ginger
freshly ground black pepper to taste (optional)

Directions

In a large resealable plastic bag, combine beef with garlic, pear, green onions, soy sauce, sugar, sesame oil, rice wine, sesame seeds, fresh ginger, and ground black pepper. Seal, and refrigerate for 2 to 3 hours.

Preheat grill pan over high heat. Brush oil over grill pan, and add beef. Cook, turning to brown evenly, for 3 to 6 minutes, or until done.

Tangy BBQ Ribs

Ingredients

8 country style pork ribs
1 cup honey
1 cup ketchup
2 tablespoons molasses
1 (18 ounce) bottle barbeque sauce

Directions

Preheat grill for medium-high heat.

Lightly oil grill grate. Grill ribs for 12 minutes, turning once during cooking. Transfer ribs to an 11x16 inch baking dish.

Preheat oven to 350 degrees F (175 degrees C). In a large bowl, stir together the honey, ketchup, molasses, and barbecue sauce.

Bake ribs, uncovered, for 1 hour. Remove from the oven, and drain fat. Coat ribs with the honey sauce. Continue baking for another 1 1/2 hours, or until ribs are tender.

Easy To Do Oven BBQ Chicken

Ingredients

1/2 cup ketchup
1/2 cup honey
1/4 cup red wine vinegar
4 cloves garlic, minced
4 tablespoons olive oil
6 cut up chicken pieces

Directions

In a medium, nonreactive bowl, combine the ketchup, honey, vinegar and garlic. Mix well, cover and refrigerate for at least 1 hour.

Preheat oven to 350 degrees F (175 degrees C).

Heat the olive oil in a large skillet over medium high heat. Add the chicken parts and saute for 2 to 3 minutes per side, just to sear the meat. Transfer chicken to a 9x13 baking dish and cover each piece well with the reserved sauce.

Bake at 350 degrees F (175 degrees C) for 35 to 45 minutes, basting with the sauce every 15 minutes.

BBQ Beer Can Chicken

Ingredients

2 cups cherry wood chips
2 (12 fluid ounce) cans beer, half full
1/2 cup dark brown sugar
1/2 cup kosher salt
1/2 cup paprika
1/4 cup ground black pepper
1 teaspoon cayenne pepper
1/4 cup vegetable oil
2 (3 pound) whole chickens

Directions

Soak wood chips in water for at least 1 hour.

Preheat an outdoor grill for indirect medium heat, about 350 degrees F (175 degrees C).

Mix together dark brown sugar, kosher salt, paprika, ground black pepper, and cayenne pepper in a small bowl. Place two half full cans of beer on a baking sheet. Spoon 1 teaspoon seasoning mix into each can. Be careful, this will make the beer foam up and out of the can.

Rinse chicken under cold running water. Discard giblets and neck from chicken; drain and pat dry. Rub each chicken with 2 tablespoons vegetable oil. Rub the remaining seasoning mix over the entire chicken, inside and out. Fit each chicken over a can of beer with the legs on the bottom; keep upright.

Drain the wood chips and place them with the coals or in an aluminum pan on or under the grill grate as directed by the grill's manual. Place the two chickens, standing on their cans directly on the grill. Close the lid and barbeque the chicken until no longer pink at the bone and the juices run clear, about 1 hour 30 minutes. An instant-read thermometer inserted into the thickest part of the thigh, near the bone should read 180 degrees F (82 degrees C). Remove the chickens from the grill and discard the beer cans. Cover the chicken with a doubled sheet of aluminum foil, and allow to rest in a warm area for 10 minutes before slicing.

BBQ Rib-eye - You Won't Believe It!

Ingredients

2 (10 ounce) marbled beef rib-eye steaks
2 teaspoons garlic powder, or to taste
1 teaspoon salt
1 teaspoon ground black pepper
2 (12 fluid ounce) cans cola-flavored carbonated beverage
2 cups barbeque sauce
8 slices bacon

Directions

Score steaks on both sides in a diamond pattern using a sharp knife. Punch the fatty areas with the tip of the knife. Sprinkle a thin coating of garlic powder over both sides of the steaks, then sprinkle with salt and pepper. Rub to get the seasoning into all of the scores.

Place steaks in a shallow dish, and pour the cola over them. Cover, and marinate in the refrigerator for 4 hours, turning steaks over every hour or so. During the last hour, coat the steaks with a thin layer of barbeque sauce.

Preheat an outdoor grill for high heat.

Lightly oil the grilling surface. Place steaks on the grill over high heat, and cook until almost burnt on each side, about 4 minutes per side. Reduce the grill's heat to medium-low, or move steaks to a cooler part, and place the bacon strips on top of them. Cover, and slow cook for 10 minutes per side.

Spread a thin layer of barbeque sauce over the steaks during the last few minutes of cooking, and allow it to cook until dry for a glazed effect.

Printed in Great Britain
by Amazon